S – R – D

THE TRAVELER'S GUIDE

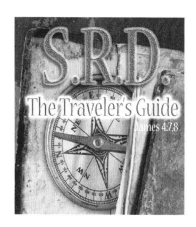

Simply Living Victoriously

S - R - D

The Traveler's Guide

This printing, May, 2009

Other books by Bruce Montroy

Winning the Inner War

Doorway to the Abundant Life

The Law of Rest

Loving God

Eyes of Faith

The River

AVAILABLE FROM

Spear Ministries, Inc.
P.O. Box 161
Prescott, AZ 86302
(928) 776-9649
smi@SpearMinistries.org
www.SpearMinistries.org

~CONTENTS~

INTRODUCTION

As a youth I found myself pretty much on a continual spiritual roller coaster, wanting to please the Lord one minute, then getting lost in doing my own thing. The battle got worse in college and the stakes were higher. A total surrender to the Lord Jesus in 1965 did so much to push me off the fence. Shortly thereafter Norma and I were called into the ministry.

The struggles I encountered after the life-changing surrender in college were never that severe, yet I saw how others were fighting the same inner war to enjoy the abundant life Jesus promised. Bible college was tremendous and I can never discount the incredible blessing it was, yet my inner itching took me toward the deeper life, the life hid in Christ. Crucified with Him.

The Lord took my path through excellent teaching on faith, deliverance, praise, inner healing, all of which were so valuable in counseling people as a pastor over 40 some years. It was in the late 1980's that my spiritual trek came together in written form, first with "Winning the Inner War," and then "The Crucified Life."

During these times of searching for every bit of help the Lord had hidden away in His treasure chest, the Bible, I was impressed with a very significant truth. Somehow the positive and negative aspects of our faith had to be combined, but in a way that prevented a negative attitude, while swiftly dealing with our adversary. We must praise the Lord in and for all things – the Word teaches that – but while we are so employed, the rascal from hell can dismantle things and derail our best efforts if we don't fight the fight of faith.

The armor of the Christian was given for a reason. No fighting leads to captivity. Yes Jesus won the great battle, but we must do the "mop-up" work of taking the territory around us. How do we fight the foe yet remain positive? Enter James 4:7,8. While putting together my first workbook for counseling, these two verses of James said it all. We must submit all to the Savior – just like I did in 1965 – for it alone opens the door to the Father's reserves.

The quick, decisive "dealing with the devil" that James offers, gives little time for the foe to distract us and lead us on wild chases. Jesus would cast out demons with a word, not many, no, just a word. The Master would run off the accuser with His authority, the same authority He gave the church. James was asking us to do the same thing. And to prevent a negative fog from settling over us, he tells us to draw near to God that God would draw near to us. Simple, fast, efficient.

So I share with you this very simple truth from as many different angles as I can, hoping that you take the simplicity and employ it and discover your very own arsenal, fit for your lifestyle in serving our King. Nothing new, but perhaps stated in a fresh way to invite you to maximize your time with the Lord while minimizing your time spent in warfare.

A special thanks to my proof reading staff and dear friends who have encouraged me through the years: Norma, my closest assistant and helpmeet for over forty years, my eldest daughter, Michele Bennett, my brother Brad, the grandmother of two of my grandchildren, Jean Alexander, our website administrator, Ronda Ehlert, and friend, Virginia Hruza. Any typos that slips past this team probably need to be included.

Chapter One

S - R - D

As a fellow traveler on this exciting journey through life, I have come across a most helpful tool that can quickly shift our focus off of that which is taking us nowhere or even worse, puts us in a tailspin. Three simple responses can stop an attack from unseen forces, calm jittery nerves, and halt obsessive thoughts.

Good intentions and extreme effort can take us in the wrong direction. Simple victory for the believer is not about frenzied activities but rather simple responses to life situations. If personal relationships are not what you desire, if career activities leave you depressed, if you feel like you're spinning your wheels, then you need to avail yourself of God's simple gift that can turn events around and begin releasing the power of His promises.

Jesus said His burden is light and His way is easy. The Father has promised to never leave us or forsake us. Throughout the down-to-earth book of Proverbs we are continually encouraged to fear God, obey Him, and our trek through life will be blessed. Therefore it stands to reason that God would provide simple steps to make life smoother.

Imagine a promise of turning everything that touched your life into something good. Father God made just such a commitment to those who have a special relationship with Him. Life is not all good and therefore the promise has special value to us when things are helplessly out of our control. We are expected to do what we can and be good stewards of what's entrusted to us; however, when everything seems to be falling apart, the one in a covenant relationship with God Almighty has a most incredible resource. Father God will turn everything for our good.

If all is good then why do we need God to turn things for our good? And of course as you look around and see the effects of the dark kingdom, you realize that life without the Lord is very hazardous – here and for sure in eternity. If you are not sure of your relationship with the Lord, please take time to read over "How can I know Jesus better," at the end of this book. The truths we're going to look at depend on entering into an active relationship with God through His Son Jesus Christ. He has so much for us, I don't want you to miss out on anything.

Let me share with you something that came to me while writing my first book, *Winning the Inner War.* We know there is a war going on inside each of us – the Apostle Paul made this very clear in Romans chapter 7. Pondering his plight, we can sympathize and are tempted to shut the book and sigh, "Well, I guess there's little hope for me if the great Apostle couldn't get his act together." Not so fast. If we quit reading before we get to chapter 8, we might feel a bit hopeless, but what was impossible for Paul in chapter 7 was the Lord's job. It is easy for God to do what He does best – be our God. Our provider.

Jesus provided a way to immobilize the sin machine. He paid the eternal price for our sin and for the whole world – past, present and future. Looking behind the scenes, God, the very God that created the Universe and everything in it with His powerful words, stepped down to earth, entered the womb of a virgin, allowed Himself to be trapped in a mortal body, was tempted as we, yet remained a perfect, holy sacrifice for sin.

The good news of the Gospel is that God Himself took our sin and destroyed it's consequences by His substitutionary death. What we deserved, He took on Himself. His plan was hidden from the devil, for we're told that had he known what the death, burial and resurrection of Jesus was all about he never would have incited the leaders to crucify Jesus.

Because Jesus paid the price for the eradication of sin, we are now free to choose not to allow sin to be our master (see Romans chapter 6). That being the case, we stand in a very tremendous place, an opportunity of opportunities. We can either look at the negative, evil, sinful mess of the flesh... the stuff that promises health, happiness and wealth... and watch as it destroys us. Or, we can look on Jesus, our new Master, and watch Him turn everything that touches our life into good. Simple isn't it? Easy? Yes, and when we look unto Jesus, the author and developer of our faith, we are giving Him a special kind of praise. It's called trust.

So here we are, traveling through the jungles of life. Sometimes it's a sunny meadow and fun picnic... other times it's a battle. The battle has been won by Jesus, yet still in our minds there are booby traps and bullets whizzing past us. It doesn't always seem like He's won the battle for us. But there is a faith tool (the

Bible) that we need to pull out of our back pack and employ the second we sense danger, depression, or disaster.

The answer is in the fourth chapter of James. He starts off the chapter by voicing some of our frustrations of unanswered prayer. He throws in a very hard to understand verse (vs.5) that seems to be saying that the Lord is very aggressively desiring our whole devotion. Then this passage...

> **Submit** *therefore to God.* **Resist** *the devil and he will flee from you.* **Draw near** *to God and He will draw near to you. Cleanse your hands, you sinners; and purify your hearts, you double- minded. James 4:7,8*

Simply put, in every situation, pause and **Submit** each detail to the one who has promised to work everything together for our good. It stands to reason that if we hold back anything from Him, that becomes a point of resistance. By not letting Him have all the pieces of our puzzle, we are saying that we can fix it. He is gracious enough to let us try. By submitting every part of an event to Father God we are declaring to heaven and earth that we believe that the Almighty God is going to perfect that which effects us.

The tremendous promise of Romans 8:28 that God will work all things for our good is conditioned on being called of God (saved), and loving Him. Can we say we love Him if we won't submit to Him? In fact, submission would be involved in being saved in the first place.

The Lord has said, "If you love Me, you will keep My commandments." I feel it is safe to say, therefore, that God's promise to turn everything that touches our life for good depends on our love prompting us to submit everything to Him. In other words, we must submit to Him the things we want transformed for our good.

> ...we must submit to Him the things we want transformed for our good.

Once we're submitted to the Father, we are in a protected space, and from this strategic position we are to **Resist** the devil, that he would flee. Because his diabolical tricks go back to the beginning of time, we, by ourselves, are no match for him. And to "slug it out" with the arch enemy of our soul is exhausting work if we try to do it on our own.

Picture a small tyke standing in front of an evil mobster, acting sassy. With little other than great self-confidence, the brat will soon be history. Now take the little one and place him behind the biggest, most powerful angel you can imagine. With the protection of the new position, there is hope for the child. By submitting first every detail of our experience to the Lord, we are actually putting the entire army of Heaven between us and harm's way.

You may not believe in the reality of the devil or his minions. I'll bet you believe in "bad vibes." or at least you can see the power of evil in our world. Yes, there is an enemy of everything that is good; a kingdom of darkness that is actively seeking to steal, kill and destroy. Even secular psychologists, that prefer to call themselves atheists, use the expression, "They're fighting their personal demons." It's as though they are acknowledging something "outside" of the person that is negative and aggressive.

I go into much more detail in *Winning the Inner War*, but suffice it to say, when we submit ourselves to Father God, He steps in to protect and transform every situation for our good. Submitting to Him is like a tag-team wrestler giving permission for his partner to enter the ring and fix things. And, imagine the biggest, most powerful helper stepping into the ring on our behalf.

To make the sandwich of protection complete, we **Draw near** to God. This is so vital. Without this step we will remain on the battlefield rather than on the mountain top with our God, in sweet communion. This is also a huge act of faith. We are leaving the details to the only One who can work them all together for our good. This is the child

> **To make the sandwich of protection complete, we Draw near to God.**

hugging the angel while the rest of the angelic band takes care of the details.

It is so easy to draw near to Father God. We don't have to **feel** thankful, but just the mere giving of thanks enters us in through the Gates of Glory. Mentally we can run into His sanctuary, His courts, with praise. There is complete protection in the holy place of the Most High God. Things all around us can be falling apart, but in this safe place, under the wings of God, we can collect our thoughts and savor His comfort. It's here, in heaven's corridors that we will be given incredible insights and wisdom for our next move. We can enter without "feelings" but our emotions will soon reflect the peace that passes understanding.

Although drawing near to God through thanksgiving and praise is so easy, we will be tempted by distractions. Like irritating "pop-ups" on our computer screen, people will want us to refocus on downers. Trying to set them straight will likewise distract us even more. So smile outwardly and inwardly slip up on Father's lap, look into His fantastic face and praise Him for working all things together for your good.

When well-meaning friends offer advice that can take us in the wrong direction, all we have to do is say something like, "Thank you, sis, for caring." Meanwhile, we can inwardly draw near to God – the source for our every need.

Now that you have the simple S-R-D formula, begin trying it yourself. When tensions rise or fears tiptoe in, **Submit** every detail to Father God, chase away the enemy (**Resist**) and **Draw** even closer to Father God.

Come with me on a travelers' adventure through the chapters ahead as we look at this "treasure" in greater detail.

Chapter Two

SUBMIT

What is the difference between an average garage sale and a good old rummage sale? At a garage sale, letting go of that item you paid big bucks for is hard... selling it for a quarter. People mill around your wares, asking occasionally, "What will you take for this?" When your price reflects your emotional attachment, they usually put the "treasure" down and move on.

At a rummage sale usually someone else marks your "precious" items at a move-it price. There is no sense of ownership. "Hey, I don't want to haul this stuff off to the Salvation Army, so make an offer." The shopper smiles as they walk off with virtually stolen treasure, a deal worth bragging about.

Enter the estate sale. What the departed slaved over and protected with such diligence is now pawed over and treated like a pile of boring debris. Photographs that meant the world to their original owners will likely be recycled in the local landfill. How sad.

Or is it a vivid reminder that only the fireproof will make it into eternity? Which, being the case, is an excellent thing to tell yourself as you seek to employ S-R-D by submitting a matter before you to the loving Father. When God asks us to submit everything to Him and His omniscient, omnipotent care, He's asking us to have a rummage sale attitude, and an estate sale mentality where we stand back and put an appropriate value on stuff.

Let's say you have a gemstone worth a lot of money but you're starving. You can't eat the jewel; but you can sell it – let it go. Your act of submitting the "valuable" to a prospective client can transform it from an inanimate article into a useable energy form. When we let go and give our situations to God we are entrusting our "precious" to the One who can do something about it.

What may hinder us from entrusting our situation to the Lord? He might do something we don't want – like ending a relationship or removing a pitfall. As a teenager, the last thing I wanted to do was to be a preacher. Yet when Norma and I gave our lives to

Lord in 1965, that's just what He led us into. Yes, it was a struggle to let go. Am I sorry? Hardly.

I still remember my grandmother saying, "But there's no money in that." She was poor all her life, and somehow thought I would make more money as a Forest Ranger, for which I was studying at Arizona State College. Okay, so she was right about the money part, however, I have enjoyed the most amazing life for just a simple kid from Phoenix. What I am saying is, when we give every detail of a situation to Father God, He will do what's best for us and actually give us the desires of our heart.

...when we give every detail of a situation to Father God, He will do what's best for us and actually give us the desires of our heart.

> *Delight yourself in the LORD; And He will give you the desires of your heart.*
> *Psalms 37:4*

God protects that which we commit to Him and usually allows us to keep it. Be assured, He will do that or give us something better. Not a bad trade.

Some of the wealthiest people in the world have not tasted the joy and peace that the Lord has given me in trade for my giving all to Him. And every believer that submits everything to the Lord can say the same thing.

Submitting things to God is both a decision as well as a mental resolve. Romans 12:1 calls us to present our bodies as a "living sacrifice" to the Lord. How do we do this? It's not by doing everything we detest. It's a lifestyle that actively seeks the Father's guidance, knowing He has our best in mind. If we have misgivings as to how much God cares about the details in our life, it will be harder to trust Him with all the pieces. Resolve in your mind that He proved His love for you in that He gave you His very own Son.

There are those that feel God loves you so much He will bring disasters into your life to teach you. He takes stuff away to make you stronger. He puts sickness and disease on you to help you grow in grace. Help. Stop. Apparently someone didn't read the Bible... What would you do to a parent that treated their children that way? Here comes CPS and some jail time. Jesus made it real clear:

The thief comes only in order to steal and kill and destroy. ***I came that they may have and enjoy life, and have it in abundance*** *(to the full, till it overflows). John 10:10 (AMP)*

The world has twisted this verse around, making Father God out to be an overly harsh parent. Why would you ever want to submit everything to someone who wants to make you miserable? I can understand why some folks resist God and submit to the devil. They are convinced that the devil wants them to enjoy life, while their concept of God is a joy-stealer. Sounds like the lie the devil sold to Adam and Eve.

Read Psalm 1. Reflect on the promise of God to make us prosperous and bless everything our hands touch. Ponder Psalm 23 or Psalm 91. Factor John 3:16 into your musings. Now, read this verse slowly and ask yourself – who wants to bless me and who wants to destroy me?

Now to Him who is able to do immeasurably more than all we ask or imagine, according to His power that is at work within us...
Ephesians 3:20 (NIV)

How could we ever trust terrorists that have vowed to destroy us? Are we in our right minds to allow an evil government to take control of our every move? No wonder some freak out when we tell them to submit everything to God – they run from the One they suppose is out to ruin them. But wait. If God is so bad, why doesn't He just throw the lot of us into hell and be done with it? Why would He give us His only begotten Son that we might have eternal life and everlasting abundance in heaven?

No, Father God is not the bad guy and we can trust Him completely. The enemy of our soul, the devil, intimidates, incriminates, badgers, provokes and in general makes life miserable. First Peter 5:8 says, he prowls around seeking someone to devour. And in contrast, God gives us His armor to protect us against this formidable foe. Which one should we resist and which one should we submit to?

In the Garden of Eden Satan pushed Eve to eat the forbidden fruit and then immediately told her that she was naked. Eve resisted God and submitted to the devil. Not smart; however, every time we take matters into our own hands before we submit them to God, we're doing the same thing. Submitting to the one who wants to destroy us is just plain dumb; submitting to the One who wants to give us the desires of our heart when our ways please Him is very intelligent.

The devil is still working hard at making life miserable for all of us. He pushes us to cling to stuff that doesn't matter. He tries to trick us into insisting on being right, to win every argument at any cost. Maybe a good definition of sin would be: Submitting to the evil thoughts the devil pumps into our mind. A definition of victory would then be: Submitting EVERY thought to Father God for His call of right or wrong.

Revelation 12:10 says the devil accuses us night and day. And imagine, this evil foe tries to get us to trust him, submit to his power plays and resist the Loving Father. Sometimes we need to hear someone yell real loud, "S-R-D," to break the hypnotic spell of this bewitching fiend from hell.

> Sometimes we need to hear someone yell real loud, "S-R-D," to break the hypnotic spell of this bewitching fiend from hell.

We can count on our adversary trying to lure us into rebelling and then with evil pleasure he "rightfully" accuses us before the One who gave His all to save and bless us.

SOWING AND REAPING

Another way to look at the vital value of submitting everything to Abba, Father, is considering the Law of Sowing and Reaping. Simply put, what you sow you will reap. Plant, by faith, every situation with the Lord and you will reap bountifully. Don't look at submission to Him as a "losing control" situation but rather as truly gaining **greater** control. He promises to work all things together for our good when we love and obey Him. So, when we plant everything that touches our life into His garden, He personally guarantees great blessings for us. Sow submission; reap abundance.

You've heard it said that you are what you eat. Diet formulas warn us that what you consume will show up one way or another. Health professionals warn us to avoid foods that will produce plaque that will cling to our artery walls. Now consider that what you don't submit to the Father in a tense situation can actually be eating you. As we submit the details of life's encounters, our S-R-D tool will take us past fretting on the negative. Fear is what happens when we hang on to plaque-causing thoughts. Let go – give the matter to Abba. Trust Him to do what right now may look totally impossible. He has all power. Solutions for our problems won't even make a dent in His resources.

There is a rather scary verse in First Samuel:

> *For rebellion is as the sin of witchcraft, and stubbornness is as iniquity and idolatry. Because thou hast rejected the word of the LORD, he hath also rejected thee from being king.* *1 Samuel 15:23 KJV*

Some view stubbornness as a good trait, and not considering God in their plans is no big deal. Behind the matter of rebellion is the thinking that the rebel know best – for themselves and for others. Allowing others the freedom to hear God for themselves is thought to be a big mistake. A controlling person has a hard time trusting God or man to make good decisions. Such a person would never want to submit everything to God, for they think they know better than He does.

Most of us hate being manipulated. Yet the pressure behind rebellion is the same force that tricked our first parents into the sin of "exercising their inde-pendence." God designed us as creatures with a free will that we might share His glory in freely loving and obeying Him and loving those around us. The arch enemy of everything that is good pressures us to rebel, take matters into our own hands, and follow the impulses he pumps into our minds via our society and polluted thinking.

Submission to Father God on a regular basis prevents the build-up of spiritual blindness and stubbornness. We will be tempted to think we know what is best for others, when in reality we don't have all the data and we can not see around the corner, much less into tomorrow. Why stoop to witchcraft-like activities where we try to make others conform to our agendas? Why not trust every detail of our lives to the only One who proved His love for us?

Submission to God, the first of the S-R-D, should be so simple. Imagine traveling to the Himalayas to hike up Mount Everest. You pay good money to hire an experienced guide. The one you pick has been up and down the mountain countless times. When you come to a place where you think you should go right but he says left, how hard is it to submit to his leading? That's how difficult it should be to trust God, the One who created us. He's been around forever and knows us better than we know ourselves. To submit every situation to Him is wise and the shortest way to get where we want to be!

The beauty of S-R-D is that we quickly move from submitting to resisting for only a **brief** change of focus. When it comes to resisting, remember: K.I.S.S. **Keep It Short Saints.**

Chapter Three

RESIST

A con man calls telling you that this is your lucky day... you have just won one of three prizes. However, you just watched a segment about this kind of scam on the nightly News so you quickly hang up the phone. Rude? Which one is being rude? The one seeking to take you to lunch, or you for resisting being his next meal? Resisting the devil can be this simple.

A caller asks you to donate to a worthwhile charity. When you tell them you need to pray about it, they go off about how crazy that is. "Just do it, don't pray." Uh-oh. When anyone wants us to remove the S from our S-R-D – resist **them**. This isn't being rude, it's honoring Father God. Do we owe pushy people a hearing? Of course not; and neither do we need to pause before we resist the devil in order to give him equal time. He's already had more than his share of time.

WWJD?

What does it mean to resist the devil and he will flee? WWJD: What Would Jesus Do? How did Jesus do this in His wilderness temptations? He didn't have a nice chat with the one who acted like he really cared about his welfare. No discussion. No detente. Jesus used the Word of God, the believer's sword. Quoting the Scriptures instantly makes us Master-minded. We need not engage in a two-way conversation with the foe determined to destroy all that reflects God's glory. After quoting the Word of God, Jesus told the devil to leave.

Sometimes, when Jesus cast demons out of people, he would tell the demons to never return. Good hygiene. Other times He sent the evil spirits out of the country. In one place the demons begged not to be sent to the Abyss. My question is why would they ask Him not to do this unless it was His usual response. I have found great relief in imitating this WWJD action, and I use a couple of chapters in *Winning the Inner War* to expand on what I feel the Scriptures teach on this subject.

I believe that we are to react to negative (demonic) interference quickly, decisively and **sandwiched** in between submission and praise. Whatever you do, don't lock horns with the enemy. That's the Lord's job. In fact, Jesus already took care of him. During this time between the verdict of Calvary and when Satan is bound for a thousand years (see Revelation 20), it works best to brandish the Sword of the Word and get our focus back on to Jesus ASAP.

I picture a child resisting input from an undesired source – fingers in their ears, humming and singing. It won't work to resist the devil by sticking our fingers in our ears, but we can sing a Gospel song or quote a favorite Bible verse. The main thing is to not allow our adversary to side track us. He wants us to focus on the negative; Jesus wants us to focus on the positive. The accuser wants us to accuse ourselves or others; Jesus wants us to look to Him for His grace that can fix any situation.

I think one of the ways King David resisted the devil's attacks was to make up new songs – the Psalms. Try resisting the enemy's attacks by making up a new song. It doesn't have to rhyme or be clever. Start describing the glories of our awesome God. Fill your mind with praise. In your singing, see the Lord of glory high and seated in the heavenlies, ruling in all His power and might. David said:

I have set the LORD always before me.
Because He is at my right hand, I will not be
shaken. Psalms 16:8 (NIV)

and

You have made known to me the path of life;
You will fill me with joy in Your presence,
with eternal pleasures at Your right hand.
Psalms 16:11 (NIV)

Resisting need not be a nasty battle but rather a command: "Leave." – followed by a Scripture or a positive praise session. See the angels of God standing by, ready to offer service for those who are to inherit salvation, waiting for you to back off so they can

---

Sometimes we can't seem to shake the enemy... Perhaps we have fallen in love with something that we can't let go of...

---

chase off the harassing foe. Picture a divine shredder ready for the angels to use to take the situation that is bugging you and mulch it into fertilizer for your miracle.

Sometimes we can't seem to shake the enemy. His talons might have hooked our heart. We're told that the fear of God is to hate evil. Perhaps we have fallen in love with something that we can't let go of – like being right, or a tantalizing lust. Poor Lot's wife. She left something in Sodom and turned to look back only to be petrified. If you sense something pulling you back, ask the Lord to help you define what it is that you need to submit to Him.

There is a danger of getting into legalism, which would be thinking we can please God by what we don't do. However, faith is a positive, submissive attitude that is willing to do whatever God desires. Whereas legalism has no power when it comes to resisting the devil, true submission to Father God does.

Sometimes the devil taunts and intimidates us, telling us we don't pray enough or read the Bible enough or go to church enough. The implication is that we don't have the power to resist him because we don't "do" enough. The truth is: Jesus did more than enough! And when we're submissive to Jesus, we have full authority over the devil. It's good to remind the enemy of Romans 16:20:

> *The God of peace will soon crush Satan under your feet. The grace of our Lord Jesus be with you.*

Psychological issues and deep habits may be connected to the enemy having a secret place in your heart. You may need a friend or mentor to help you sort through questionable issues. I say, when in doubt about an activity, give it up to the Lord. Sometimes we can't think clearly about the right or wrong of an

---

...deep habits may be connected to the enemy having a secret place in your heart.

---

issue because we have too tight a grip on it. Nothing can substitute for the peace and joy that comes from a full surrender to Christ.

When you are resisting the enemy and he fights back with incessant haranguing thoughts, realize this is one of the devil's servants. You have complete authority over him, but you have to use it. Like a policeman witnessing a crime, the crooks don't come over and willingly submit to him. He has to exert his authority. "Stop in the name of the law."

We can exert our authority over harassing spirits like this:

"In the Name of Jesus Christ I bind you, spirit that put that thought of ____ in my mind. Leave me now and do not return.

If you have difficulty getting the victory over obsessive thoughts or inner voices, I suggest you read my book, "Winning the Inner War." You can download it free of charge online from our website, or contact us at the address in the back of this book for a free hard copy.

How long does it take to resist the devil? Most of the time a short "Go, in Jesus' name, and don't return" is all that's needed. Then immediately switch your focus back to enjoying sweet fellowship with the One who loves you the very most.

The longer you take to resist the devil, the less likely you will actually resist him. The D in "Draw near to God" can also stand for Drive. Drive away – speed off. Run. Get into the Throne Room and the Mercy Seat as fast as possible. And while entering His presence, let His angels minister to you as they did to Jesus following His temptations.

The Father will send angels to minister to you, and they will likely be "unawares." He may send people with words that sound superficial because they appear to discount the scary battle you just escaped. But if their words are positive and faith based – lap them up like a bowel of milk before a hungry kitty. Don't get distracted by who God chooses to use, just allow their positive encouragement to thrust you faster into the Lord's presence. This is no time to impress anyone with how tough your battle was.

The faster you pass from resisting a negative attack to enjoying a big party of praise, the faster your miracle will hasten to you. We untie the Father's hands by eliminating doubt and double-mindedness. When we decisively resist the enemy and then speedily dine at God's thanksgiving table, people will remark at the sudden change in our countenance.

I have a strong belief that the tyrant that troubles us with sickness and disease will have to take a lot of his maladies and exit stage right. God designed our bodies, when in balance, to heal themselves and resist all manner of infections and diseases. This balance, however, requires the "perfect peace" the Father promised to those that stay their minds on Him.

Thou wilt keep him in perfect peace, whose mind is stayed on Thee: because he trusteth in Thee. Isaiah 26:3 (KJV)

Chapter 4

DRAW NEAR

What a promise: Draw near to God and He will draw near to you. The gates of heaven are unlocked. The doors of His sanctuary are open 24/7. Saint or sinner – come to find His grace – His salvation. But come. Imagine placing a call to heaven and not having to push number 1 or 3 or being put on hold. Heaven is standing by, ready to take your call.

Why is it we know the Lord can read our every thought and even distinguish our motives, but we feel we have to have some kind of special audience for Him to hear us? Do we need to see a bright light or have an angel glow with a faint red appearance? The One in Whom we live and move and have our being knows what we are thinking and as instantly as we turn our focus on Him, we've already had His attention.

What's faster than the speed of light? The speed of thought of course. Now consider that the God who fills the Universe knows our thoughts here, on planet earth, as well as if we were on the far side of the Galaxy. He knows when our focus shifts from irritation to praise. **He is well aware when our feeble efforts at faith reach out to Him.** He created us for fellowship and when we seek that intimacy with Him, His joy begins to flow into us. You will sense with

---

> He created us for fellowship and when we seek that intimacy with Him, His joy begins to flow into us.

---

your feelings His presence. He was always present, it's just that now we're aware of it.

He gave us emotions as a monitor. Remember Romans 8:6? When we feel separated (death) it's because our focus is on the fleshly things that produce separation from God's glory. When we shift our focus on to the One who IS Love, His essence will manifest in us – in our mind and emotions. So how do you feel? In His presence is fullness of joy and at His right hand are pleasures forever more.

So what do we say when we draw near to God? We are told that without faith we cannot please Him and that we need to believe not only that He exists, but that He rewards those that diligently seek Him. What about starting with describing how incredible He is. Paint a praise picture of the One who spoke the Universe into existence. Recount to Him some of the fantastic miracles He's done in your life. Thank Him for being a rewarder – your blesser.

Perhaps I should make mention that you might have a bit of a problem with this part of the tools for our travels because you are still pretty sore about a time in the past when you felt God let you down. Could we step back and objectively look at this matter for a minute.

Every problem that hits us has two sides awaiting our response. The negative forces desire to kill, steal and destroy us at every turn. Our foe watches, waiting for us to falter and then rushes in with accusations – of us and of those who have hurt us. The mature believer knows we must forgive others, so we do. The reason, however, that we may feel we have to keep on forgiving and dealing with old hurts is the accuser, who loves to bring up the past and get as much milage out of every hurt that he can.

Old issues, where we thought the Lord let us down, actually were occasions to prove our trust. The loving Father has promised to not allow things to get too rough for us and that He will always provide a way of escape. We are told He won't tempt us with evil, and what the enemy means for evil, God will turn into blessings and deliverance for us and others. When we are tempted to feel that God is letting too much come our way, taking an S-R-D timeout will give us insights and stamina and hasten the promise of Romans 8:28.

Because every problem has two opposing sides waiting for our response, we cannot pamper our ego or please the wrong side by whimpering. Why wallow in despair when we can reach for a solution? Why settle for pity when victory is only an S-R-D away? As we draw near to the One who loves us the most, His presence dissolves confusion and questions.

At the first remembrance of an old stumbling block, an offense we used to nurse, we will be far better off to submit the old hurts for healing rather than trying to figure it all out. Our analytical side wants to "make sense" out of things. Our judicial part desires that the guilty one "pays for what they did." Do not recycle old hurts. Give every aspect to the only One who can truly bring good out of bad.

When we submit old hurts, poor reactions and even our cloudy suppositions to the Father, resist the accuser, and then draw the grace of God into our memory banks, we can actually renew our mind. The Lord will turn our handicaps into a super highway to His courts as we dare to trust Him via praise.

We have our own ideas of how life should go and if we are prone to be a take charge person, we can resent interference that takes life in a different direction. My main question is more of a health issue. Has the burying or festering of past disappointments helped or

> The Lord will turn our handicaps into a super highway to His courts as we dare to trust Him via praise.

hindered? If it left a mine field, booby traps that spring on people close to us, then it may be time to turn disappointment into diamonds.

I used to love it when Superman would take a lump of coal and squeeze it into a diamond. What the man from Krypton cannot do, the Lord of Glory has promised to do. There is no time limit, to my understanding, for the guarantee of Romans 8:28. As best you can, roll out the records and tell the Father how you feel about each one. Then roll them back up and offer them up to Him as one of the most costly sacrifices you could ever give. When you do this, get ready for the most fantastic series of life changing events.

WHAT DO WE GET IN RETURN?

Imagine a huge field covered with solar panels, continually following the sun's path across the sky, drawing in the energy of our sun and converting it to clean electricity. How hard is that? When we were created by God, He made us to be converters of His glory – Son panels. As we draw near to Him, the incredible presence of the limitless God fills every crevice, every empty spot, with His divine energy.

A clean energy source is what the inhabited world desperately needs. And those around us likewise need people in their life (us) who aren't drawing endlessly from them. Yes, as a society we are inner-connected, but you know what I mean when I say some people are a real drain. When we draw from God what only He can give, we radiate out to those around us something that can act as a "demo" to induce or encourage them to draw from God.

On the contrary, if people see us as a continual drain, emotionally drawing their energy, they will have little excitement about reaching out to our God. So there's a double blessing in drawing near to God. First for our own spiritual receptors to gain the life we need for true fullness, and secondly to have more than enough to share with those around us that are so in need and have no clue which way to turn.

So what good do we get from God drawing near to us? If you have ever walked closely with the Lord, as David of old, to feel estranged even a little causes your soul to ache and cry out for His living water. Imagine being Adam or Eve before the fall, having the Lord come down in the evening and walk with you in the incredible Garden of Eden. The palmist said, "In Your presence is fullness of joy and at Your right hand are pleasures forever more." Sounds like a pretty exciting thing for God to draw near to us.

If you haven't had a time of closeness with the Master, you may have reached for some of the common synthetic, empty placebos the world offers. Some seek to scratch the inner itch with things that can never satisfy. Most addictions, I feel, are monsters that cry for more and more while rendering less and less relief from inner cravings – cravings that only the One who made us can fill. The sad thing is, worldly placebos cost big bucks and have awful side effects. God's sure cure for our inner itches is free. It makes sense and "cents" to draw near to the only One who really cares and can supply everything we need.

Our society is so crazy over sports, weekend RV trips, and a host of activities that are quite fun while they are happening, but can leave us broke, empty emotionally, and sometimes in the hospital. Drawing nigh to God gives Him **permission** (a social grace of a caring God) to draw near to us. We will sense His presence with

> Drawing nigh to God gives Him **permission** (a social grace of a caring God) to draw near to us.

the part of us He made just for that purpose. When we try to fill it with something else, it doesn't work. When He's a part of sports, trips and recreation we gain maximum benefit.

Imagine friendship with the One who knows all, loves us more than we love ourselves, and has all power. He's never left us, nor will He ever turn against us. His presence is more wonderful than having all the money in the world. He is like a continual festival. In His presence is joy forever more.

Sometimes I have such heavy questions I want to ask Him, and when I feel His presence, the questions dissolve in wonder. There is nothing, absolutely nothing, that can compare to His drawing near to us. If you have not experienced this yet, you have the most incredible experience awaiting you. If you have, then you want it more.

WHAT IF HE DOESN'T DRAW NEAR?

Why might the Lord not draw near to us? There were times in the Bible when a prophet or king could not seem to get God's ear. Why?

> *But your iniquities have separated you from your God; your sins have hidden His face from you, so that He will not hear.*
> *Isaiah 59:2 (NIV)*

Couple this with the declaration in Romans that whatever is not of faith is sin. As we get bogged down with making excuses to the accuser, the devil, and justifying our actions to everyone, we can get self righteous. Like Job in the Old Testament, we can think better of ourselves as we compare how much we do for God and how we are not like so-and-so. If we give more credence to thoughts of worry and fear than the promises of God, it will put us in a bad position –

shrinking faith. Worry is actually a form of pride that thinks we can handle life better than the Creator.

The Word warns that God resists the proud but gives grace to the humble. Therefore, when we submit everything to the Master, we are on the right track. This submitting leads to repentance and a fresh application of the Blood of Christ. Being cleansed afresh, we have a new confidence to resist the devil. And then as we draw near to Abba, His grace exalts us, lifts us up and refreshes and renews us as nothing else can. We get our second wind and we can run and not be weary. The breath of God's Spirit lifts us as we stretch our wings out in surrender.

NEED VERSUS DRAWING

It's so easy to say, "Lord we need You," and still remain in our mess. The fact is, the whole world needs Jesus. God's promises must be received. To enjoy the favor of God, we must move past the awareness of our need to action. We must draw near to God. We need to draw Him into our situation by faith.

According to Romans 4:17, God calls into being that which does not exist. In 1 Timothy 1:7 (NASB), we are told that God's administration (how He works) is by faith. When there is nothing, the Father speaks and it comes into being. To imitate our Father, we need to speak that He is meeting all our needs **before** we see or feel them being met. In the spirit realm, they are already met. We S-R-D not to "get" God to meet our needs, but to celebrate that the answer is on the way.

When our needs launch our S-R-D response, we step out of need into the arena of faith by drawing near to God with our words. While it is true when we say, "Father I need You," it does not move us out of our situation into His provisions. "Lord Jesus I draw You into this situation right now," changes our focus off of our need onto Him. The more we speak by faith, the faster S-R-D works to change our state of affairs. **Our focus must draw near to God and draw from Him.** It is up to us to change the frustration of "need" into the dynamic of drawing.

It's been said that God is not moved by our needs. If He were, there would be no needs and we would all be in heaven. Our panic and fears do not trigger intervention by the Lord on a consistent basis. Yes, He is moved by our needs, but not necessarily into action to eliminate them, but to make provision for those who will draw Him into their life by faith.

> *Therefore I say to you, all things for which you pray and ask, believe that you have*

received them, and they will be granted you.
Mark 11:24

We can surely express our needs to Father God, but
faith takes us a huge step further. We are called on to
take a great big giant step into the unseen control
room of the Universe where miracles are produced.
God prophetically speaks that things **are** (exist) when
they are in the process of production, or soon to be.
Recall from Psalm 139 that the Father writes down in
His book all about us before we're born. And Romans
5:17 says we are called to rule in life through Christ.
Our words can aid in the production of our miracle,
when we, like our Father, speak faith. This is co-
rulership. We are to be a team.

To sum up this line of thinking, drawing near to God
will include speaking like He does. When He gives us
a promise, we speak that back to Him. For instance, in
the middle of a bad situation we draw near to Him by
quoting 1 Corinthians 10:13 that He will not let us be
tempted beyond our ability to resist, and He will make
a way of escape – an exit. This builds our faith (faith
comes from hearing the Word). It pleases Him
because we are honoring His Word.

Allow yourself to get carried away with reciting His
incredible promises because the more you do, the

faster the conveyor belt moves in His factory that is producing your miracle.

Chapter Five

SLUGGISH RESISTANCE

Sometimes S-R-D just doesn't seem to work. What is wrong? Most likely we need to apply the rest of James 4:8, 9 and verse 10:

> *Cleanse your hands, you sinners; and purify your hearts, you double- minded. Lament and mourn and weep. Let your laughter be turned to mourning and your joy to gloom. Humble yourselves in the sight of the Lord, and He will lift you up.*

Dirty hands? Is there something you are doing that you know full well you should not be doing? Is there something you know you should be doing and are not?

Double-minded? Wanting God's best and the world's best at the same time? Oops. Speaking faith one minute and negative or worry words the next? Barking at people for messing everything up and then saying we believe in Romans 8:28? Yes, being double-minded will employ S-R-D for a moment and then stop the process by getting sidetracked with taking matters into one's own hands.

Laughter? The verses (above) warn: *"Let your laughter be turned to mourning and your joy to gloom."* There is a good laughter, but James is talking about the kind that mocks or discounts the things of faith. Such laughter is not of God and is actually working for the foe. It will require repentance for them to turn around and begin serving the Lord. Once they turn, the Father exalts them, lifts them up, fills them with real joy and then they will have a good reason to laugh.

Mocking and sarcasm are difficult traits to break. James is basically saying they will need to see how harmful these seemingly benign responses are. Ishmael mocked Isaac and it cost him his inheritance and a huge rift began that still is odious today (Gen 16:11). We are to edify others and help them draw faith and love from the Lord; inappropriately laughing at others is a tool of the accuser, our adversary. We sure don't want to be doing his job. If S-R-D doesn't seem to be working, look for signs of mocking or inappropriate laughter.

Negative laughter may also be seeing everything as a big joke – people's feelings, obligations, your promise? More concerned with how others let you down than how you fail to follow through on what you know you should be doing? There is a worldly joy that is not righteous. I believe that James is talking about such a party mentality, always having fun, ignoring the still small voice of the Holy Spirit. If we do our own thing, when the chips are down and we try to S-R-D as a sort of lucky charm, sorry, it won't work. Covered guilt hinders the Lord's power in our life.

Pride? How can we tell if we have a problem with pride? Do we get upset when we think God has blessed someone that we don't think deserves to be blessed? Do people accuse us of being prideful or judgmental? Do we argue about little things? Are we easily offended? Do we look down on others?

> *But He gives a greater grace. Therefore it says, "God is opposed to the proud, but gives grace to the humble." James 4:6*

Who is as proud as the arrogant person who thinks they don't need the Lord's help? Who is as humble as the one who does not want to do anything without the Father's participation? Notice that God gives His grace to those who humble themselves. The Lord told the Apostle Paul when he petitioned heaven for the removal of a thorn in his flesh, that the answer was His grace. He equated His grace with His power. God gives this grace/power to those who humble themselves under His lordship, and S-R-D is a fast way to do just that.

We humble ourselves in the presence of the Lord when we submit everything to Him. This requires trust and faith and it honors Him in a special way. When we resist the one who has set his kingdom against the Lord's, we are coming against the father of pride. When we cleanse our hands, we will quit trying to take what doesn't belong to us; we will stop trying to force life to go the way we think it should.

> We humble ourselves in the presence of the Lord when we submit everything to Him.

I feel James is saying the discovery of these negative traits in our life will prompt a brokenness that will draw in the power of God. Repentance will come easily. We are not to stay in the place of conviction, but allow the Lord to lift us up, clean us off and make us single minded.

I don't want us to bog down in this chapter with negative issues. But, we need to be aware that if S-R-D does not work as good as it should or has, consider spending some time alone with the Lord to take inventory. Avoid taking the club from the enemy and giving him the night off as you bonk on yourself for being human. That gets us nowhere. Rather see yourself entering the throne room of the Lord of Glory. Lay everything down at His feet.

If you come across something that you are not quite ready to let go of, you have probably found your hindrance to the flow of God's power.

What James is getting at in chapter 4, verses 8-10 is there are times when our spiritual life needs a shock. We get into ruts of ho-hum and same-o-same-o. We can slowly cool off to the point where we begin allowing behaviors to go unchallenged. Things we used to jump on quickly and confess as sin, we sweep under the carpet. When the carpet resembles a mountain, we will have little confidence resisting the enemy. Probably, because we know we have not honestly submitted everything to the Lord.

When you miss the closeness of the Master, know that His awesome presence is just a heartbeat away. Purposefully empty out your pockets of the trinkets and weights that so easily beset us. It's honesty and trust that He desires of us. Ask Him for help to step back from that which has hypnotized you and made you numb. Sensing His glory and anointing is worth any price.

Chapter Six

STRESS

Behind so much of the temper flare-up we see today is stress overload, thanks to our society. We heap plans and expectations on ourselves and others, even God. Deadlines are everywhere. Detours abound. Traffic congestion, accidents and time delays appear to hinder us at every turn. Mishandled stress can trigger a chemical reaction in our bodies that can make our journey harder. Stress hormones are known for causing a host of diseases.

As we gain momentum in our pursuits, our energy is linked to accomplishing our objectives. Derailed efforts can leave us feeling totally exhausted. At such times we are prone to pamper ourselves – so much for the old diet. When the scale scolds us for our "escape from reason," guilt from a lack of discipline adds to our stress level. The key is to deal with stress when it is small and manageable – not with food.

Some may zone out in front of the television. Does getting lost in artificial situations and even documentaries solve the issues that led to our stress build up? I doubt it. If we're not careful what we allow into our minds via the media, we might find new stressors piling up. Television should be enjoyable entertainment, not a weight that pulls us down. Expecting TV to provide relief from stress, a job that our God is supposed to do, can end up being a form of idolatry.

Personal relationships can add a lot of stress to our life. Friends are supposed to encourage us and lift us up; but what if they are bogged down with their own stress? And what if we try to find answers from others and instead they begin trying to draw from us? What if we both have holes in our bucket? The beauty of S-R-D is that we have a good bucket to draw living water from the Lord's well of hope and wisdom – enough for our needs and those who come to us!

Some people take life so seriously. Everything is a big deal. The Nightly News makes them so mad, but they can't do any thing about the injustices. Such simmering may be overlooked but it can contribute to major health problems and at the same time etch away at faith. If we can catch ourselves as we begin to get upset and immediately S-R-D, we can actually be part of the solution – intercession! Our world needs people of faith and prayer to stand in the gap, and the rise of indignation may be the Spirit calling us to prayer rather than simmering.

What can we do about the world's problems? National leaders won't listen to us. The Master's call is not for us to worry or try to fix everything, but to pray with thanksgiving. When we resist the negative pull of problems and instead flow in positive, thankful prayer, we are immediately on the Father's side. We are cheerleaders, of a sort, invoking the angelic watchers. The choice is, do we want stress producing reactions to pull us down or do we want godly responses that contribute to the Lord's victory?

Stress results from putting far too much stock in our efforts and way too little on God's prayer answering power. Worry results from seeing scenarios from the perspective of a practical atheist – they live and act like there is no God. Are we factoring the Father into our plans? Is it possible that what we are trying so hard to make happen is not the Lord's will? We don't dare submit it to Him because we know what He'd say. Sounds like a call for the S in S-R-D.

A real sobering thought I've had a few times when I'm in the middle of a "big deal" is: "What if the Lord called me home before this got completed?" We huff and puff and sweat and get all in a tizzy when things get blocked... but what if the trumpet blew and we were gone? Out of the picture? Who's big deal would it be then? With this attitude, it is easier to let God be God and get on with enjoying His presence.

The Lord allows life's tests to see how we will respond. He knows what we will do but He enjoys it when we relax, let go, and trust Him to work it all together for our good. We're the ones who need to know our limits and where we need to draw lines and make fences. There is a "breaking point" we never need to discover if we will deal faithfully with the small steps leading up to the brink of disaster. The beauty of S-R-D is that it works with small issues and most times prevents them from growing into big problems. Every issue is seen as an occasion and reminder to run into His presence.

> *He who is faithful in a very little thing is faithful also in much; and he who is unrighteous in a very little thing is unrighteous also in much. Luke 16:10*

Faithfulness to keep in close contact with Jesus makes it so natural to reach out to Him for help when difficulties start to emerge. There is a confidence that comes when two people are close. If you haven't experienced this before, you will find fantastic, instant relief when, instead of worrying how you are going to fix the problem, you simply draw Jesus into the situation. S-R-D keeps the line of communication wide open. We don't have to run off to a meeting or call someone for advice. Wisdom and confidence usually arises from inside us, where the Holy Spirit dwells, before we have a chance to get sidetracked by fear.

Some of the "deepest" communication we can have with the Lord will be over the small things and can lead to insights and understanding of the secrets of our heart. This is true stress relief. The Spirit can unmask control issues before they sideline us with frustrated attempts at controlling things and people.

Why do things have to fall apart before we turn to the Lord for help? Is it written somewhere that we are supposed to suffer stress buildup until we get to the breaking point? Does it take massive stress overloads to wake us up? Isn't it wiser to pause, lay every detail of our lives at the feet of Jesus, chase away the stress master, and pull in the Father's favor?

Stress can be a helper if we allow it to trigger our S-R-D response when we first sense it. Can you feel in your body when stress begins to build? Sometimes it is as though we want to see how much we can take before we slap the mat and give up. Here is another way to look at life's stresses. How much can the Lord and I master? At the first sign of stress, the least little bit of pressure buildup, S-R-D, thereby pull the Lord into the ring. This is the trigger to the promise of Isaiah 40:28-31:

Have you not known? Have you not heard? The everlasting God, the LORD, the Creator of the ends of the earth, neither faints nor is weary. His understanding is unsearchable. He gives power to the weak, and to those who have no might He increases strength.

*Even the youths shall faint and be weary, and the young men shall utterly fall, but those who **wait** on the LORD shall renew their strength; they shall mount up with wings like eagles, they shall run and not be weary, they shall walk and not faint.*

What does it mean to **wait** on the Lord? Probably many more things than both of us can come up with. But, obviously, it would mean we must factor the Father into our stress management. Maybe we are still trying to gain a trophy so others will know we are special. Forget it. Haven't you seen the old trophies at garage sales? Who cares about old news? Yesterday's heroes are pushed aside by today's headlines. If we really want recognition for being special, go for the Lord's commendation... "Well done thou good and faithful servant. Enter into the joy of the Lord."

Spiritual stress management is walking in the Spirit. Sometimes we have the freedom to run; other times we cautiously walk, placing one foot in front of the other. Stressful situations require we slow down and make sure of our next step. When we have been hurt or our energy is depleted, we are wise to use the Spirit and God's promises as a spiritual walker – looking before we put our weight down. Leaning into Jesus.

Why the caution? In high stress times our wisdom juices are generally lacking and our fight or flight hormones are typically surging. We need some restriction on our actions – a delay mechanism – like taking time to Submit all the stressors to Father God. It is always wise to pause for some time with our Savior for wisdom and refreshment. There is a time for "fight or flight," but at the wrong time it will increase our stress. S-R-D reaches for the stress solution.

Stress reminds us to reach out for the Master's hand. I'm not talking about Sunday religion. This is every day walking and talking with our heavenly Father. This response is so practical and when we develop confidence in the Lord's concern for the small details of our life, we will prevent many bigger problems.

Properly dealing with stress and its accompanying problems is what separates out successful, enterprising people. Overcomers use the wisdom that comes from being able to step back from an issue and objectively analyze. If we are all tensed up because of some kind of pressure to succeed (internal or external), we will be less able to focus or think creatively. And when it seems most important, it is extremely hard to loosen our grip for even a second. This puts way too much stress on our system – body, soul and spirit.

If we train ourselves to pause for refreshment, we'll sense new energy, fresh insights, and our old friend, creativity, dropping by with neat advice.

Chapter Seven

TIME DELAY

So then, my beloved brethren, let every man
be swift to hear, slow to speak, slow to wrath;
James 1:19 (NKJV)

There is a need for a time delay between when a thought pops into our head and we speak. James is asking us to slow down. Ponder before we reply. Listen more and talk less. And it would seem this verse is linking talking too much or too fast with anger. Fast words, flash anger.

"Swift to hear," but who are we listening to? Some of the thoughts that come to us are from the accumulated wisdom we have gathered over the years. Some cliches and empty slogans are not worth repeating and those around us are probably tired of hearing. We need a time delay to sort through our many thoughts,

and if we're slow enough to speak, we will have the good sense to throw out the worthless thoughts.

In this traveler's guide, we are looking for potential snares that will hinder our journey. One of the greatest pitfalls in relationships along the path of life is the spoken word. How many times have we wished we could take back hurtful words? Sometimes we speak before we have all the facts. Wouldn't it be great if we had a tongue depressant, a governor for our motor mouth? If we would but take some time to **submit** our thoughts to the Lord, chase off the accuser of the brethren, and then draw God into our thinking, we could pave over many of the pitfalls in our path.

It has been said that the only exercise some people get is jumping to conclusions. When we feel we have to talk fast, we will find ourselves grabbing for the next word... and this is precisely where we find ourselves most vulnerable to the enemy. He can slip harmful thoughts into our mind, and if we have not developed a time delay, a mental filter, we can do a lot of damage in a short time. Instead of jumping to conclusions and grabbing for the next word, our best exercise will be to do a set of S-R-D's!

Counting to 10 has helped some people manage anger. Numbers are nice but they do not have the power that we can draw from God. Time delays and changing our focus are good tools but for maximum value, we need to draw positive input from the All-wise Savior. Remember, we're promised that when we draw near to God, He will draw near to us. Instead of counting, try submitting the details of a problem to the Father. Taking the time to list every detail helps strengthen our focus.

Where did Jesus get all His incredible wisdom? He said that He would only say what the Father told Him. When things were happening all around Him, He was drawing near to His Father for eternal wisdom. We can do the same thing.

A key to making the S-R-D time delay effective is to ask questions. We can ask others for more information, but the real source for wisdom is to whisper a prayer and ask the Father for His input. When we draw near to Him, we will receive answers and insights that will astound us and help rather than hinder relationships.

> *But if any of you lacks wisdom, let him ask of God, who gives to all men generously and without reproach, and it will be given to him.*
> *James 1:5*

Doesn't it make more sense to seek wisdom from God rather than get into an argument with someone? In a frenzy of too much talking we can say things we don't mean. How is that? Like I said earlier, the enemy sticks words into our mind and if we are not careful we can blurt out hurtful stuff that we can never erase. In calm reflection we would be quick to say we didn't mean to hurt them, but without a time delay, our mouth was moving faster than our brain!

What if we find our self in a heated discussion with someone who really needs help? Does it make more sense to try to out talk them – speed talk – or take a moment, go into another room and get some life-saving advice? What if this "other room" is in your temple, your mind? Taking a "time out" to check in with the greatest Counselor will make all the difference in the world. The S-R-D time delay will provide us with the best answers – and it's free.

I started this chapter off with James' admonition to be slow to speak. Interactive "live" broadcasts today typically have a few seconds of delay just in case some caller says something offensive. Many times I wished I had a 24 hour time delay before I opened my big yap. Enter S-R-D. When we pause and run our thoughts through the Father's x-ray machine, we are more prone to spot hidden bombs. The heat of a moment can fog our windshield and we need some time to see clearly, hear Abba's cautions, and gather winning wisdom. But there is a problem.

We live in a "shoot from the hip" generation. Wisdom is not exalted in our society, rather it's how fast you can come back with a "cool" answer. Mock fast enough and you get your own TV show. But have you noticed how many of the loose-lip hosts have had to make apologies and some have even lost their jobs due to flash fast words that lacked discretion.

Sometimes we feel pressured to jump into a conversation and speak our mind rapidly or we won't be heard. Ever notice how most of the time our "great insights" aren't heard anyway? Some of our quick-draw comments aren't thought through and we end up with egg on our face. Better to obey James wouldn't you think?

What is going on with jabber-boxes? Some people talk non stop. The writer of Proverbs says, in so many words, you can't avoid getting tripped up with much speech. Father God promised through Isaiah, *"In quietness and confidence is your strength."* I wonder if weakness, and frequent infirmities is linked to talking too much. Are you a jabber-box? Am I one? We probably both are at one time or another. Okay, you probably aren't, but I used to get paid the big bucks to talk non-stop for 30 minutes or so.

How can we bridle the old tongue, which, being in a wet place is prone to slip? Like the sign reads at the swimming pool, we too need a big sign that states: "Walk, Don't Run." We need a good clutch that has to be engaged before we put our mouth in gear. You know what I'm going to say don't you.

So how do we develop an internal time delay mechanism? It will require more dialogue with the Lord Jesus who lives inside us. David said he set the Lord before him; we can too. What if we pictured the Lord walking beside us, or seated in the car next to us – as close as He says He will be: "I will never leave you or forsake you." To me this is "praying without ceasing." Talking everything over with Him. Because our mind goes constantly, we need it to be doing something constructive while we're trying to be patient.

Maybe we can periodically be still and listen; but when we just can't shut up, we can talk to the Master in our inner temple – **first.** If we talk to Him first it says that His opinion or attention is most important to us. I think we can train ourselves to listen more by asking questions. It's easier to be quiet when we're listening for answers.

There is a huge problem in families when the individual members feel free to say whatever pops into their head. Imagine the amount of damage being done by the indiscriminate believer who "speaks their mind" when their thoughts, like Peter's in Matthew 16, are really from the troublemaker. Ugh! We need a time delay so we can ask, "Father, is this great insight from you or my wounded ego?"

> There is a huge problem in families when the individual members feel free to say whatever pops into their head.

Here's a novel response for those who love to talk. What if you are having a discussion that is getting hot and heavy and the great insight, the show-stopper pops into your mind. You say to your listener, "Hey, I just had this thought, tell me if it makes any sense or if it's off the wall..." instead of doing, like many of us, speak first and think later. Humbling ourselves before another for their consideration just might evoke the Lord's gift of grace. And nothing says we can't do an S-R-D out loud. It would show those within listening distance that we know we're not infallible – which we might otherwise be accused of.

Now for the nastiest of accusations leveled at believers: "You're judging me." Don't you hate it when they come off with that and all you wanted to do was to help? What if their sharing was a cry for help and we shot back with a judgment – judge, jury and executioner. A time delay could be as simple as asking for more information in a tone conveying compassion. During "heavy" times, silence can say you are giving serous thought to a matter. In your mind you are carefully going though S-R-D and listening for God's wisdom.

Paul, in First Corinthians chapter 4, said he wouldn't judge anything before it's time and without getting all the facts. Interesting, because in the next chapter he tells the church to ostracize the fellow living in sin. So, he must have done something to get enough of the facts to make such a pronouncement.

Let's face it, there have been times in our lives when we needed someone to hear from the Lord and confront us with a news flash that was less than uplifting. Nathaniel's "Thou art the man," spoken to King David, turned things around. But the prophet heard from the Lord. So many need bold prophets today to lovingly confront their sin without being fleshly and/or omitting solutions. If ever there is a time to be slow to speak and double check with the Lord before opening our mouth, it's when the message is intended to sober up the listener. Recall how Peter really thought he was sticking up for Jesus when in actuality he was speaking the thoughts the devil put in his mind.

If the moment to impress the world with our gigantic insights passes because we took the time to S-R-D, be assured of this – the world is probably better off. Timing is everything. Jesus said He had things to teach the disciples but it wasn't the right time – they could not receive it right then. That might be the case with our wisdom. We have to trust the One who gave us the insight to also coordinate the circumstances for its delivery.

Lag time – thinking about how we sound to others – might prevent us from whimpering and complaining about things that don't appear very important to others. If we are trying to impress someone by saying something silly, a mental time delay might help us save face. Pausing to consider what we say can prevent us from throwing cold water on someone with a pride problem. The S-R-D pause can turn our focus from saying something negative, to giving words of encouragement. There's nothing like a timeout and discussion with our Guide.

There are several other responses that require a time delay if we are going to be mature and successful.

FAITH REQUIRES PATIENCE

For ye have need of patience, that, after ye have done the will of God, ye might receive the promise. Hebrews 10:36

The answer to our problems can be so close and our faith can be chipping away at the mountain, but if we quit too soon, it is all for nothing. Faith does not work for the double-minded person. What do we need when our faith is just about expended... we are just about ready to quit? We need a time delay. We need something to keep our faith working on the problem while we change our focus and get some refreshing. Before throwing in the towel, S-R-D.

We need time delays for our words, but time delays when we are waiting for answers to prayer can take their toll. Patience is the muscle of faith but delays can sap our faith muscles of their strength. The key to strengthening patience is focus. Have you noticed how time flies when you are having fun with good friends and how slow it crawls when you are caught in traffic? Life has plenty of detours and delays so we better get some focus changers. What about talking with your best Friend?

When we focus on a required response from men or machines (or ladies getting ready for church), it seems like forever before our patience is rewarded. The beauty of S-R-D at such times is that it helps pry our focus off of frustrations and puts it on the God who calls us to "be still" and know He is in charge.

I think of the big trouble that the young, inexperienced King Saul got into when he "forced himself" to offer the forbidden sacrifice instead of waiting patiently for the priest. Samuel was late – shame on him – but Saul's impatience got him into trouble just the same. In contrast I think young David would have taken his harp and written a praise song to Yahweh, the Lord strong in battle. Saul was more concerned with the fearful "soldiers" going AWOL rather than

> ...when we reach out to Father God, our Provider, instead of allowing irritation to boil over into improper responses, we win.

considering the God of Gideon who cleaned the enemy's clocks with a handful of guys.

If only Esau had taken his supposed starvation through S-R-D he wouldn't have fallen for his brother's duplicity. I'm sure mom would have made him a pb&j sandwich before he actually died of malnutrition. The point being, when we reach out to Father God, our Provider, instead of allowing irritation to boil over into improper responses, we win. The hand of God is rarely moved by our needs, otherwise there would be no needs in life. No, He is moved by our faith and faith grows with proper focus.

The dynamic of focus can be seen when we do physical exercise. When I do my daily 30 minutes of recumbent bike riding or meandering down the endless road of the treadmill, focus makes the difference. For time to slow to a snail's pace, just exercise. If I watch TV or an interesting DVD, time passes more quickly. If, however, I read a book while pedaling, it requires more focus and the time flies by. Good focus – time flies – patience is a snap.

Chapter Eight

SOUL HEALING

The simplicity and power behind S-R-D is the finished work of Christ Jesus. His death, burial and resurrection performed everything needed for mankind to enjoy God's full plan and incredible abundance. To discount His work on the Cross is to make a huge mistake. It puts us outside the effectiveness of the Kingdom of God. The tools He gives to the traveler are inseparably linked to the Risen Christ.

We've been specifically told that if we are in Christ Jesus we are a new creature:

> *"Therefore if any man be in Christ, he is a new creature: old things are passed away; behold, all things are become new."*
> *2 Corinthians 5:17 (KJV)*

It is understood that the "all things" does not mean that your bank loan disappeared or that your bad grade in math mystically transposed into an "A." The charges against us and against those who have hurt us have been legally (in the spirit realm) taken care of. This must be the basis for living our new life in Christ rather than believing that some of our memories are the exception. Even what people did to hurt us, yes, even the life-changing events, are all put into God's transforming machine of Romans 8:28. Whatever we consider to be outside this "made new" promise can nullify the Word of God, like Jesus said in Mark 7:13:

"... thus invalidating the word of God by your tradition which you have handed down; and you do many things such as that."

The tradition of "getting even" implies that God is not to be trusted with full justice. Sometimes we can't forgive ourselves. Frequently we feel that what someone else did to us can't be let go of until they pay for what they did. We call this closure. It should be called negating the Word of God.

We must renew our minds by the Word of God rather than trying to warp the Word because of our "experiences." Nothing in our past should hinder us in the present from doing the perfect will of God. Every supposed hindrance must be treated as a land mine – for when anyone treads on it there is a blow-up.

So, what happened to the old hurts stored in the deep recesses of our subconscious mind when we got saved? Can our subconscious mind declare "king's X" and off-limits to the renewal? Perhaps deep down we feel that unless so-an-so apologizes or "gets theirs," justice will not be served and if we let go of what they did to us we'll be aiding and abetting the enemy. Such thoughts think little of the Law of Sowing and Reaping, that it will take care of the offenders. Perhaps a lack of swift justice for those who've hurt us helped formulate such a belief.

So many things change the direction of our life. An auto accident, sickness, natural catastrophes, parents moving, divorce, bullies, molesters – the list is virtually endless. In fact, every day affects our tomorrow – this is the Law of Cause and Effect. We can't change the past, nor the effect it has **had** on us to date. But, we can participate in Father God's program of renovation, recycling, and renewal for tomorrow. When we give to Him all (or as many pieces as we can) of our life, He will transform it into what will bless us most and please Him as well.

The fact is, when we were saved, all the spiritual issues concerning us were reset. Any and all "physical" manifestations that resulted from what we sowed in the past were put in a state of change. Our spirit was instantly born again, but our mind needs to be renewed to the changes. And, our physical arena is conforming to the new reality – sometimes slowly, occasionally quickly, and maybe never until we get to heaven. Romans 8:28 guarantees that the Father's power will transform even our mistakes, physical as well as spiritual, for our good.

Science has helped us with "outside" verification that even our genes can be altered by what our mind perceives as reality. Imagine combining a mind renewed on the Word of God with the unlimited power of God that works within us. Anything is possible. God's power freed the Jewish slaves from Egypt and fed them for 40 years. The dead have been raised. Blind eyes have been healed. Literally all things can become new.

But what about our past? We can't travel back in time and change history. No, and we don't need to. What has been done has been done, but how we see it is everything. Perception can produce faith or destroy it. We've all heard stories of how two different people went through the same horrific situation and one was better and the other was bitter. Focus is the difference.

Because bad perceptions of the past tend to discount the "new creature" promise, our minds must be renewed. This is where S-R-D comes to the rescue. By submitting every painful memory and disappointment to Father God, we are turning on the converter of Romans 8:28. We are actually asking Him to turn our painful perceptions into His viewpoint.

> **By submitting every painful memory and disappointment to Father God, we are turning on the converter of Romans 8:28.**

God sees the death of the seed as the birth of the plant. He watched His Son be crucified knowing that soon He would be sitting with Him at His right hand in glory, surrounded with the joy of the Lord, and bringing many sons and daughters with Him. The Father's focus is always on our winning:

> *But thanks be to God, who always leads us in triumph in Christ, and manifests through us the sweet aroma of the knowledge of Him in every place. 2 Corinthians 2:14*

The Father sees our success. How else could He work all things together for our good? When we replay negative memories, it increases the incidence of similar or worse situations. Remember, Romans 8:6 warns us that the mind set on the flesh is death. This is why the apostle cautioned us to think on positive things:

> *Finally, brethren, whatever is true, whatever is honorable, whatever is right, whatever is pure, whatever is lovely, whatever is of good repute, if there is any excellence and if anything worthy of praise, dwell on these things. Philippians 4:8*

Philippians 4:8 is the secret to why he could say he had learned how to be content in any circumstance (verse 11). We must focus on the Father's fix rather than humanity's failures – past, present and future. And our faith in the Lord's goodness will hasten the process of transforming our raw materials in a miracle.

Take the worst atrocity that ever was – the crucifixion of Christ – and consider it before you exclude yourself and your painful perceptions from Romans 8:28's power. The pains we've endured in the past are not to be discounted, nor glorified. Rather we need to allow our mind to renew our perception of them, by faith, into diamonds produced by God's grace. Our "right now" can be compromised if we allow ghosts from the past to haunt our inner sanctuary.

Something I've not come across in the many books I've read on psychology and counseling is why we need the "R" in S-R-D. The accuser of the brethren is harassing us 24/7. And if us, then others also. He uses partial truth and twists it to produce his diabolical conclusions. He may even seem to care about justice as he goes off about these mean people "getting away with it." Don't be fooled – he hates us as much as he hates them. He is the tormenter and he will seek to destroy anyone who will agree with his twisted "evidence."

Circumstantial evidence can get a conviction from a jury if they don't know all the facts. So fully expect the accuser to bring up stuff that you dealt with long ago, forgave, confessed and let go of. The reason old issues soured in our memory banks was due to a lack of all the details – as with the crucifixion of God's Lamb. Peter was so upset that Jesus would be crucified, but knowing all the facts, we glory in the announcement! "All the facts" includes the Father's excellent plans for our good.

When you were made a new creature in Christ, any old wounds were transferred to the "Cross Claims Department." The accuser wants us to reopen cold cases and pretend that the blood of Jesus was not sufficient to take care of the past. To play with such thoughts is to insult the Spirit of Grace and keep the "case" in litigation, forestalling God applying the Law of Sowing and Reaping for those outside the reign of

> The accuser wants us to reopen cold cases and pretend that the blood of Jesus was not sufficient to take care of the past.

grace. When the case is closed, justice will be served and the details that concern us will be transformed into good for us.

A most valuable time to S-R-D is when old memories surface for whatever reason. Seasons of the year, old friends, pictures, and a host of other things can trigger old memories. I think that as some new engrams are being laid down in our brain they bump into old ones triggering old memories. Maybe. Who knows. But for sure if it's a negative memory and you don't immediately S-R-D, you'll get mad all over again, slip into a funk, or play with pity. But, glory to God, if you S-R-D, the old can be renewed. And if the accuser was trying to get you to"solve" a cold case, he'll think twice before a repeat performance.

The D in S-R-D will act as a catalyst in empowering Romans 8:28 to transform old hurts into gold. When we "draw near" to Abba, He is free to show us how He was with us through it all and how He has and is using it for our best. Such a season of enlightenment will sweeten our fellowship with the One who sticks closer than a brother. Our love and trust will overflow when we see with the eyes of faith the wonders of His love for us. Amazing boldness will result as we realize that He will never leave us or forsake us and that He is protecting all that we commit to Him.

I don't ask you to trust me on this one. No, I want you to try it yourself with the next sad, negative, hurtful, horrific or gross memory that bounces center stage in your mind. Grab the thought and stick it in your S-R-D machine. Grind it up and expose the stinker to God's incredible grace. Now pack that renewed critter back into the annals of your mental library. Try it. Taste and see that the Lord is Good. Trade your sorrows for His joy.

Chapter Nine

DIRTY WORK

How much of a threat is the devil to believers? We are warned not to give him any opportunity (Ephesians 4:27). What do you suppose that means? First Peter 5:7 tells us he roams around seeking someone he "may" devour. It appears that we have to give him permission to chew us up. How do you think we do this? The enemy has to tap into our authority – our faith.

Recall Romans 8:6, *"The mind set on the flesh is death..."* When we get sidetracked by our focus on negative things, we are opening the door to the enemy's advancements. All he has to do is to create a distraction, a diversion, like criminals robbing a bank in an old western town. Once our focus is negative, he can slip fear thoughts into our minds, and we will personalize them. Worry weakens our faith and opens the door to distrust. Pondering alternative plans is not necessarily bad, unless such focus takes us into fear and worry. It is much more rewarding to ponder God's promises.

The devil can't force us to be manipulative or hostile. If he did force us against our will, then we would be virtually innocent, such as a hostage forced at gun point to commit a crime. Our foe wants us to be legally in trouble with the Lord, therefore he must trick us into taking his evil suggestions and making them our own. You have no doubt had weird thoughts pop into your mind and of such a gross nature that it shocked you. "I would never do that," you say to yourself. Absolutely. The adversary is "fishing" for you with his worms of wickedness. Some gullible people act on the temptation thoughts and as soon as they do, the sin is their very own.

> The enemy has to tap into our authority – our faith.

The deceiver's greatest trick is to make us think we need his help. For instance, a spirit of fear has to trick us into thinking that if we are anticipating the negative, we won't be caught off guard. Maybe you have fallen for this snare. The negative person would say, "At least I won't be disappointed." But because the rule of faith is, "As your faith, so it will be, " negative thinking produces greater and greater problems. Plus, it cuts one off from the promises of God.

Because the enemy needs to convince us that we need his "helpers," his temptations will sound like they have our best interests in view. If we are ignorant of his devices, we will be sitting ducks for the enemy's offers of manipulation, hostility, anger and a host of other coping devices he hawks as survival equipment. When believers get bound up they can act just like worldly sinners. Paul called these "carnal Christians" and I think we've all spent some time there.

The question many have is, "Can a Christian have a demon?" If the person means, "Can a believer be possessed?" I would ask if they mean "owned by a demon"? I believe we can only be owned by either the Lord or the enemy, but believers can be sidelined or even taken captive, like a P.O.W.

AVAILABLE FOR LEASE

I saw a sign the other day that said the property being developed was available for lease. I thought how sometimes we have signs the devil can see that tell him we're available for lease. If we can only be owned by the devil or the Lord, it still remains possible that the unsaved can flirt with Christianity or the Christian can flirt with the devil. The sincere believer only wants to be owned, leased, possessed, inhabited and indwelt by the Lord.

Some folks throw the term "deliverance" around rather flippantly as though the devil can pull up in front of our house with a bus full of demons and crash our party. It does appear that he has and can take out a lease on backslidden believers and make them a halfway house. Maybe so. But how does one get rid of such an infestation?

If we use our authority and chase off the demons that have moved in, what do we do with the empty house? Jesus warned us that a house so emptied is subjected to a return visit, and the previously evicted spirit is liable to bring along seven worse critters with him – perhaps for protection. Not a good thing.

I'm concerned when a person requires frequent "deliverance." Could it be that they need better house hygiene? The issue, as I see it, is that the enemy has to either trick us into focusing on negative things or to somehow convince us that we need what he's offering. The prodigal son was sure that the glitter of the world was way better than what his father's farm had to offer. Drugs, illicit sex, and a host of other contraband can be dressed up and sold to unsuspecting, hurting individuals as something they need. To keep the "7 worse" away, we must be more convinced that Jesus is the one we need filling our heart house.

Before salvation we were all under the devil's thumb. Romans chapter 6 makes it plain that there is no middle "DMZ" ground where we are basically our own person. We were under the devil's authority before salvation but now are under Christ's after being born again. Simply put, we were the possession of the enemy before salvation and now we are the property of King Jesus. We were possessed by the prince of darkness; now we are totally owned, body, soul and spirit by Jesus.

> *Or do you not know that your body is a temple*
> *of the Holy Spirit who is in you, whom you*
> *have from God, and that you are not your*
> *own? For you have been bought with a price:*
> *therefore glorify God in your body.*
> *1 Corinthians 6:19,20*

The believer can not be owned or possessed by two opposing kingdoms; however **we can be so harassed**

that we may not know the difference. That sure doesn't sound very comforting to me. The mind set on the flesh will produce all sorts of death. Romans chapter 6 warns us to not go back under bondage. To determine if the person is owned by Jesus, why not try S-R-D? The fastest way to be sprung from the enemy's war camp is to submit each thought and situation to Father God. Resist the foe in the name of Jesus. Draw near to Abba and allow Him to cleanse, refresh and restore you.

The problem I've seen with someone freshly rescued from the enemy's "house arrest," is re-enticement by the adversary. He got them once by stinking thinking – he'll try it again and again. The solution? S-R-D must become second nature. It works because God is God and He has all power. The Almighty God will not refuse the one who comes to Him in Jesus' name, as long as we're not holding one hand behind our back.

What bugs me to no end is the thinking that we are virtually helpless victims of the kingdom of darkness, and that evil spirits can pounce on us indiscriminately any time they want and "possess" us. The foe has to talk a believer into submitting to bondage. Not a hard job when we're carnally minded and want to be fooled. But it's a real tough sell when we want to please Father God most of all.

I've had sincere believers say they felt they picked up a spirit at such and such a time or place. No hitchhikers. None. Don't pick up anything that distracts or diminishes the Word of God or your love

---

The solution? S-R-D must become second nature. It works because God is God and He has all power.

---

for Jesus. And here's the key to staying full of the glory of God and enjoying the fruit of the Holy Spirit – immediately when you sense the least bit of negative anything – negative thoughts, emotions, lusts, hate, anger, depression, revenge, greed, jealousy, covetousness, egomania –

IMMEDIATELY S-R-D...

What can trick us so fast is the nightly News or gossip or seeing an unjust plight or happening. Any event that triggers our ire needs to be passed through the Father's S-R-D screener – His spiritual X-ray machine. We're to look for terrorists bombs. If your anger is from God He can then direct you to the proper steps to take as you draw near to Him. Yes, there are times to get upset. But it can also be a trap from the accuser, the bully, the one who wants us to take matters into our own hands. No, we must put everything into Jesus' hands and then do what He leads us to do. Ecclesiastes informs us that there is a time for just about everything, so what we need is the Lord's timing.

Do an experiment. The next time you catch yourself getting upset at the News broadcast, do a quick S-R-D. Make sure you run off the accuser. Then listen to hear if Abba has any take on the matter. He might give you an incredible insight to share with others. Maybe an article to share with the readers of the Spear Ministries daily online devotionals. We always enjoy fresh victories and spiritual insights.

The way we learn from life is to see it from the Father's eyes. The enemy would have us shoot from the hip. Many are wired to shoot from the lip. Abba wants us to lean not to our own understanding but to acknowledge Him in all our ways and He will direct our paths. And we know His path is life – abundance – blessings – health. In His presence is incredible joy.

But aren't there some hard cases where a believer needs deliverance? As long as we are clear that the believer is not "repossessed," but has an issue with submission, okay. A demon can not own a blood bought believer. And if the saved individual is backslidden, then their only hope is to stop sliding and start submitting – to Father God, not the enemy kingdom. If they refuse to submit to God, then I truly doubt their "conversion."

If a person with demon problems is not ready to submit to Father God, share with them what we have written in this chapter. Ask them if they can spot any false help the enemy has offered. You can probably pick up some hints when they describe the bondage they struggle with. S-R-D their responses to clear your own thinking. Emphasize there is no "neutral ground" between submitting to the Lord and submitting to the enemy. And of course, a good question to ask them is, "If cooperating with the deceiver is not working for you, are you at the point of trying the Lord who loves you more than you love yourself?"

The plan of attack with someone who has serious demonic control over their life (P.O.W.) is to teach them that there is no "middle ground" where they are on their own, and can do their own thing. If they are not submitting to Father God, they are operating by fleshly principles that will only take them deeper into harassment and torment. They do not have the luxury of coasting, insisting that they are not so bad without Jesus being the Lord over their life. If Jesus isn't our Lord, then the prince of darkness is. And the only way out is submission to Jesus and receiving His provisions – His blood bought provisions.

Jesus gave a much overlooked illustration about repossession that we mentioned earlier. The individual that gets "delivered" yet remains empty will get repossessed with seven worse demons. What was He saying? Jesus commissioned His disciples to cast out demons and then fill the empty houses – by teaching them to surrender to God's Kingdom. New ownership. New Lordship.

We need to teach true believers to draw the Glory of God into their house (their body, soul, and spirit). No demon in their right mind (if they have one) will hang out in the presence of the Glory of God. Psalm 8:2 (NIV) tells us that even a child can chase off the enemy with praise. Instead of giving the devil attention he so desperately loves, give Jesus the preeminence He so rightfully deserves. Get the believer to switch their focus off of fleshy matters and on to the Living God. From coping devices to drawing from the living Christ.

To return to the metaphor of a P.O.W. camp, we must be rather frank and honest. Our "will" gets us trapped in the enemy's camp and it takes the submission of our "will" to get out. Recall how the guy with a legion of demons ran to Jesus and fell at His feet. Even that many demons can't override a person's will. The Apostle Paul shared in Romans 7 of an inner war that he was unable to win. Was he possessed? Certainly not. Was he in a battle? Absolutely. His conclusion was (8:6), that because of what Jesus provided, there was no condemnation, no overpowering bondage, but all he had to do was to switch his focus on to Jesus Christ.

If the person who needs "deliverance" is not willing to take this new lifestyle approach, we are actually doing them a huge disservice by chasing off the enemy. Jesus said 7 worse can join the "re-possessor" when he comes back to fill the empty house, and we surely don't want that. I've mentioned this several times because I think it is so important to realize before we begin casting out demons. We must not reach for short-cuts with those who just want "relief" without submission to Jesus as their Lord and Savior.

Do not cheapen the grace and provision of God by giving the enemy credit or focus. If simple S-R-D doesn't work, it's most likely because the person will not "S." They have submitted to the kingdom of darkness and they are refusing to submit to God Almighty. We must not discount the Gospel for these folks. Besides not working, it will actually push them further away from truth.

For believers to have continual problems with demonic forces is an indication that they are in desperate need of renewing their minds on the Word of God. They need discipleship and being held accountable to take every thought captive. We must not excuse their mental laziness or lingering lusts but give only one option – a new walk.

> Do not cheapen the grace and provision of God by giving the enemy credit or focus.

We have no other "quick fixes" or "drive-thru" deliverance. If they are unwilling to make their inner sanctuary an unfit habitation for darkness, we have no other options. To try to make their misery less intense without the proper cure is to insult the Lord of Glory, Jesus Christ.

Let me say it again. Deliverance without salvation and submission is dangerous. Our response with a believer who has demonic issues and won't submit to Father God must be to pray for the Holy Spirit to bring them to conviction and repentance. They are not ready for a solution. "Feeling good" needs to come from focusing good. That's right – S-R-D.

Chapter Ten

HEARING FROM GOD

Hearing the voice of a loved one is so valuable. We watch on the News as a family gathers around a television screen and video conference with their soldier in Iraq. Lovers talk for hours, just drinking in the sound of the one who loves them most. I've heard of some playing a recorded phone message over and over just to hear the one they love. Is it any wonder the sincere believer longs to hear the voice of God?

Ponder this picture we're given in the book of Revelation:

> *Look. Here I stand at the door and knock. If you hear Me calling and open the door, I will come in, and we will share a meal as friends.*
> *Revelation 3:20 (NLT)*

Friends talk. Remember at the Last Supper when Jesus said His disciples were friends? He's knocking.

Can you hear Him? If we open the door He will come in and eat and fellowship with us. He's promised that where two or more of us get together in His name He will be present. The fellowshiping Savior will talk to us.

The watchman opens the gate for him, and the sheep listen to his voice. He calls his own sheep by name and leads them out. When he has brought out all his own, he goes on ahead of them, and his sheep follow him because they know his voice. John 10:3,4 (NIV)

True discipleship includes seeking direction from the Lord Jesus. The Old Testament prophet said...

Your ears will hear a word behind you, "This is the way, walk in it," whenever you turn to the right or to the left. Isaiah 30:21

The New Testament promise is for a personal guide, the Holy Spirit, who will lead us and instruct us:

But the Helper, the Holy Spirit, whom the Father will send in My name, He will teach you all things, and bring to your remembrance all that I said to you. John 14:26

The third person of the Trinity will be in us, teaching us and imagine, He will tell us whatever He hears.

But when He, the Spirit of truth, comes, He will guide you into all the truth; for He will not speak on His own initiative, but whatever He hears, He will speak; and He will disclose to you what is to come. John 16:13

One of the distinguishing marks of being one of the Master's sheep is hearing His voice.

I have other sheep that are not of this sheep pen. I must bring them also. They too will listen to My voice, and there shall be one flock and one shepherd. John 10:16 (NIV)

My sheep listen to My voice; I know them, and they follow Me. John 10:27 (NIV)

Hearing from the Lord is so vital, yet some say the Lord never talks to them. Others talk like they and God have endless hours of flowing conversation. The verses we've just shared make it clear that we should expect the Father, Jesus or the Holy Spirit to speak to us.

Many tell of how the Lord spoke to them when they were busy doing something other than praying. I've had this happen. It's exciting and enlightening. But what if we need to gain clear direction from the Lord but our mind is rather busy with a bunch of "zooming" thoughts? S-R-D.

As we **submit** ourselves quietly before the loving Father, the One who wants us to seek first His kingdom and His righteousness, we can expect Him to give us direction. The **resisting** of the interfering enemy is very important. Chase him and his minions away in Jesus' name. Sometimes I ask the angels of God to clear the area around me of all interfering entities – principalities and powers.

Drawing near to God then becomes a soft, quiet time when we still ourselves before Him. Perhaps see yourself bowing before His throne as is described in Revelation. Softly praise and thank Him. Thank Him for directing your life and leading you in paths of righteousness for His name's sake. Then be silent. Wait. Be still and know that He is God.

Sometimes the Lord will speak audibly, but this appears to be rather rare. In John's gospel when the Father spoke audibly the people thought it thundered. His voice scared them. He knows best how to communicate with us, His friends. Expect His thoughts to sound and feel much like your thoughts.

Often I ask a very simple question, one that I know the answer for, and that doesn't offend Him. I ask, "Father, are You here right now?" Of course He's always with us, but it gives an opportunity for our spirit to tune into His voice. Listen to His voice as it will sound like your voice. If you get any weird thoughts, stop and S-R-D again, with a little more time spent on the R.

If after a while you "sense" nothing, thank Him for guiding your path. Spend some time pondering passage from the Bible that "pop" into your mind. You will likely soon sense His direction with a certain confidence that is the result of specifically seeking Him.

Notice what Jesus said when Peter gave his famous pronouncement in Matthew 16:16,17:

And Simon Peter answered and said, Thou art the Christ, the Son of the living God. And Jesus answered and said unto him, Blessed art thou, Simon Barjona: for flesh and blood hath not revealed it unto thee, but My Father which is in heaven. (KJV)

Peter didn't hear an audible voice from heaven telling him these things. He assumed the thoughts were his own. We may think what we're hearing is our own "wishful thinking" but check it out with the Word of God and S-R-D. Do the "thoughts" include hope? A promise? Do the thoughts draw you deeper into seeking the Father's face?

> We may think what we're hearing is our own "wishful thinking" but check it out with the Word of God and S-R-D.

The Apostle John warns us to not believe every spirit but to try the spirits to see if they are truly from God. I suggest that every "voice" be taken through the steps of S-R-D. We need to keep in mind that the Lord desires us to lean on Him for guidance and not our own thinking. Yes we were given a mind, but not to "do our own thing," but for fellowship with the Master.

We are more accountable, however, when we hear from God if we're not willing to obey Him. Why? Because we can't claim, "I didn't know!" If the preacher tells us something, we can dismiss it as, "he's just a man." If the Bible tells us something, we can write it off as hard to interpret. But when we know God has clearly spoken to us and told us to do something, we can end up in a fishy predicament like old Jonah if we disobey.

While we are on the subject, it is important to not try to live on yesterday's direction. There are some instances in the Bible where yesterday's direction got the slow-to-obey people in deep trouble. Recall the Children of Israel trying to go into the Promised Land the day after they said, "no." The important thing is to lift up our plans and previous "words" and pass them through the S-R-D light.

Some of the thoughts that pop into your head will be put there by the Holy Spirit, your guide. How can we be sure? S-R-D. Some of the prophecies given in a service might sound as intended for us. How can we know for sure? Don't despise the prophet but examine everything. How? That's right, S-R-D.

I will instruct you and teach you in the way which you should go; I will counsel you with My eye upon you. Psalms 32:8

Chapter Eleven

BUT WHAT ABOUT...

Some might ask...

If we're always submitting everything to God won't that make us a robot? An unthinking drone?

When we are in a pressured situation our release of adrenalin and other chemicals can actually cloud our best thinking. You may have done something real dumb out of panic. What takes place when we S-R-D in a tight spot is the flow of godly wisdom. Mental clarity and boldness results. We will actually make our best decisions following S-R-D.

In fact, when on autopilot we will tend to snap at those around us when pressures build. We will resent suggestions by well meaning friends. We may even pull back from social contacts or hold back advice when it is most needed. Rather than being a robot, when we take our thoughts through the analysis of S-R-D, we can actually become a messenger for the master. Consider His words to Jeremiah:

...if you extract the precious from the worthless, you will become My spokesman...
Jeremiah 15:19

How on earth do we ever extract the precious from some of the awful circumstances of life? As we S-R-D negative situations, we trigger the Father's involvement so fast it will amaze you. Peace and faith will flood your entire being. And seemingly out of nowhere will come wisdom and answers you had never considered. You will hear yourself saying words of life. You will literally become a spokesman for the Lord. You will be blessed beyond your imagination and others will be helped. Healing will flow and miracles will take place right before your eyes. How do I know? I've experienced it. Also, I have had many others tell me how Abba has so blessed and used them.

Don't I have to feel like doing this S-R-D stuff? Won't I be a hypocrite if I don't really believe it or want to do it?

Actually, we will be the bigger hypocrite if we don't S-R-D. Once we've been made aware of these simple, easy steps to take to turn the gross into glory, we will actually be the bigger hypocrite every time we complain about how bad things are when we didn't S-R-D. We could have changed bad into good but instead we pouted like a little brat or acted like an ostrich and stuck our head in the sand while those around us needed our help.

Feelings are a monitor of what we are focusing on. So change your focus and your feelings will change. There is a truth that offends the worldly wise. We don't have to understand something to enjoy it. I can't cook worth a wooden nickel but man do I ever enjoy what a good chef prepares.

I know so little about computers, the internet, cell phones, and the equipment I'm surrounded by. And there are a few things that I've never gotten around to reading up on, yet I enjoy them. I say that some day I'll read the manual and enjoy them even more. So it is with the things of God. Jesus said He kept some of the best stuff from the scholars and revealed it to the children. Lord I'm a child – Your kid. Teach me more about S-R-D and how it can quickly help others.

Isn't it negative to resist the devil? I thought we were supposed to stay as positive as possible.

I want you to stay as positive as possible. "As possible" being the key phrase. I agree that our society and most folks individually are way too negative. There is a little matter though that we have to deal with – we are surrounded by problems. Negative stuff is encroaching on our little "kingdom of self" continually. Our only hope is to have a "negative converter" that is guaranteed to work all things together for our good.

The process of the flow of energy back and forth from positive to negative is how we heat our homes, cool our cars and make our computers buzz. The fun part is harnessing the flow so it works for us rather than against us. What S-R-D does is precisely this – and faster than anything else ever could because the God who holds it all together insures that it works. Every dynamic situation can be harnessed to provide us abundant blessings – every one.

This is more than positive thinking – it's positive living. It is how Jesus intended us to live when He promised that His way was easy. This is what Paul had in mind when he said the Lord always leads us in triumph.

Consider the incredible, almost unbelievable promise of Jesus:

> *And He said to them, "Because of the littleness of your faith; for truly I say to you, if you have faith as a mustard seed, you shall say to this mountain, 'Move from here to there,' and it shall move; and nothing shall be impossible to you." Matthew 17:20*

Wow. Can you believe this? Now for another unbelievable promise, but more of a negative nature:

> *But let him ask in faith without any doubting, for the one who doubts is like the surf of the sea driven and tossed by the wind. For let not that man expect that he will receive anything from the Lord, being a double-minded man, unstable in all his ways. James 1:6-8*

Almost scary isn't it. Our enemy only needs to distract us and get us to doubt. We end up sinking like Peter on his water walk. Now for the good news. Ready?

When we S-R-D at the first sign of trouble, and then continually, as a battle ensues in our minds over partial evidence, our focus is strengthened on the Promise Giver. If we ponder "the facts," fleshy advice will float into our minds (guess from where). As we play with doubt-thoughts, our faith is watered down. A thought of doubt that flashes into our minds will not cancel out our faith if we take it captive– if we S-R-D it as quick as we realize what's going on. Scattered seed doesn't grow instantly.

There is a time period for us to respond to thoughts – I call it lag time. Paul said if we judge ourselves we will not be judged. The key to walking in faith is to learn how to handle the negative thoughts that are thrown at us. If we can retrain our minds to quickly S-R-D, we will not miss a beat – plus it will help us stay close to the Lord. One thing you will discover: His fellowship is sweeter than anything you can imagine. I would trade the whole world for it. S-R-D makes us feel so close to the One who made us. As we witness miracles all around us, we will show the world our Father's love.

But if this S-R-D stuff is true, how can I ever say to someone "I'm sorry I can't help you?" How can I

ever feel that there is nothing I can do, that it's out of my hands?

Of course you know I cooked up this objection. I hear people say this a lot – "There's nothing I can do." Oh really? I thought Romans 5:17 said we are to rule in life through Christ. We can always pray, but that seems so benign to most. What if we clear the air around a situation and our friend by saying the steps of S-R-D out loud? It will most likely precipitate a course of action that can change things.

The discouraged person suffers from tunnel vision. Talk about thinking inside the box – they are in a little dungeon. Our assistance as an angel, a messenger of God, a spokesman for the Lord, can throw open the doors and if they have the restraints loosed from their emotional wings, they can fly with us above the situation and enjoy a new perspective as Father God squeezes another lump of coal into a diamond for His beloved. Didn't Jesus give us the keys to the kingdom – to bind and loose? Bind the negative with words of faith and loose the captive to enjoy loving on our God with us. This is true group worship.

If the person we're talking with is being oppressed by the enemy, our "R" action can help clear the way.

Perhaps they will see what was going on and join us in pushing the discourager out. With the monkey off our back, we can all see a lot clearer.

Isn't it rude to talk positive with someone going through a hard time? Aren't we supposed to weep with those that weep?

This may be one of the reasons we don't encourage those going through a difficult time. Jesus wept at the tomb of the friend He would soon resurrect. Yes, we are to weep with those who weep. My question is how long? I've been involved with many grieving families. Being a pastor since 1969, I've had my share of marrying and burying experiences. What I've noticed is that even at a wake, someone will crack a joke or mention some trait of the deceased that was just plain funny. All laugh. What happened to the grief? Oh it's still there but no one thought it rude to interject a positive comment.

We try to comfort others with how "They are in a better place." Some pretty silly remarks are also made at the bedside of one in traction, facing an unknown future. Is it any more rude to weep with them and then lift their tears with yours to the Father who keeps them in His bottles? When we lift the problem up to the Problem Solver and then resist the enemy, we are pushing the negative out of the picture, at least temporarily. Even when we make terrible decisions and incur accidents based on simple stupidity, don't we all really desire less gobbly gook foolish talk and more solutions and hope for a fix?

Rude is to know where the answers are and refuse to share the secret because someone might think us "too religious" or super spiritual. It's not about us. It's what does Jesus want me to do or say right now. Start with S-R-D and He will show you.

This taking every thought captive to Christ and always S-R-D-ing everything gets real old, real quick. Isn't there an easier way to get the same results?

Actually, I believe we will experience fewer and fewer times where we really need to S-R-D and more times where we just draw near to the Lord in praise. The resisting part can get real old real fast and if we are not careful to keep it to a minimum, it can sidetrack us. The things that steal our joy and drain us emotionally need the quick application of this part of the Traveler's Guide. It is the fastest way to get back on track, lift our focus, and build our faith. If it seems to bog down, we are probably spending too much time on the resisting part.

The reality of S-R-D needs to be compared to the mental exhaustion that comes from arguing with yourself or the accuser about the stupid comments you made at the party or what you should have said to the nasty clerk. It's the negative put-downs (of our self and others) that wears us out big time. Wouldn't it spare us much mental turmoil if we dismissed the negative chatter in our head? We get nervous, fearful, prideful, angry, and depressed when we think too long on things that pull our focus off life-giving matters.

I think we ponder our mistakes to look for excuses as to why we messed up, or to build up walls to prevent our getting hurt in the future. Both are dead end streets. Why others did what they did is their business, but trying to figure it out will probably give the devil two-for-one. It is so much better and far more refreshing to submit every detail – yes, even our failures – to Abba, get the accuser off our back and then in the sweet sanctuary of His throne room gain the wisdom and refreshing only He can provide.

Won't S-R-D become just another formula? Another legalistic routine?

There is a huge challenge before all of us to keep life as simple as possible, yet fresh and interesting. Some of life is a formula and we think nothing of it: brush your teeth, take out the garbage, change the oil and a host of other mechanical duties. When was the last time you felt warm and fuzzy when you mowed the grass?

The biggest challenge to keep things fresh is that of personal relationships and worship. What a task for church leaders: present timeless truths in vital, fresh ways. Let's face it, sometimes we pray or sing worship songs and our heart and mind are somewhere else. It takes effort to **focus** in on some aspect and quicken our attention for good.

The beauty of S-R-D is that the first two parts can be cut and dried. A formula for confessing our sin as part of our prayer is thought to be okay. And the Lord's Prayer in Matthew chapter 6 includes dealing with the enemy: "deliver us from the evil one" (New King James Version). **Every** prayer needs to submit to Father God first! Formula? Maybe. But a very vital formula, just like H_2O!

The beauty with this formula is that the D, Draw Near to God, can be totally spontaneous! We can allow just about anything to trigger worship – even awful, ugly things can be turned into praise that our God reigns and He is fighting for us, turning all things together for our good.

Our challenge is to apply S-R-D in every circumstance and come out on top of the situation, heart full of praise, and the strength that comes from waiting on the Lord.

Chapter Twelve

TESTIMONIES

Does submitting every situation to Father God, resisting the devil that he might flee and drawing near to Abba produce results? Here's what some have shared.

* * * * * * *

I have been raised in a Christian home. I had been taught some very wonderful things that have shaped me into who I am today. However, I noticed as I was growing up I was fighting a battle that I could not see and I did not know how to fight. I was taught to love my neighbor as myself, be kind to one another, basically the golden rule was what I was living by.

When you are fighting a battle and you don't have the necessary weapons to win it, your efforts can seem so futile. It was after I got married in my late 20's that I really began to have trouble with inner battles. Things were happening to me that were beyond my control. For example I was getting my feelings hurt on a regular basis and I did not know what to do about it. I was living the way I had been taught and it wasn't working. I would hide away by myself for hours, crying and praying, hoping for a breakthrough all to what seemed like no avail.

My struggles were with bending and blending with my husband. I always felt like I was doing the right things and thus felt justified in all of my actions. My actions, I would find out later, were those of someone who was defending and protecting herself; after all, if I didn't do it who would. I noticed that my husband and I were becoming very alienated from one another. We were newlyweds, and where was the bliss that I had always heard and dreamed about – you know, the happily ever after.

I was becoming sadder and more frustrated each day. I found that I often was too troubled to even speak about these issues. I had reached the end of myself. After several months of crying myself to sleep pretty near every night as I was still searching for the happily ever after, it began to set in that, that would never exist. I felt hopeless. What an empty feeling. I contacted my pastor, and made an appointment with him, hoping he could give me an answer for my confusion. He had me go through two of his workbooks, the first one was Winning the Inner War and the second was The Crucified Life. These books changed my thinking and changed my life. I learned that a lot of my thinking was stinking. I had always prided myself (and my husband can attest to this) that I was trying to live the righteous life, therefore I must be doing everything right, therefore, I most of the time, was probably right. My poor husband; I always made him out to be in the wrong and me in the right.

I really thought it though. I learned that many of the thoughts we have are not our own. That when we have a thought we need to first find out where it came from and really ask the Holy Spirit to show us. If it is not from the Lord then it is from the enemy and we need to arrest it and lock it up and throw it into the abyss. This was foreign to me. But I noticed that this started to work immediately. Sometimes I would feel tired of checking every thought, but eventually I noticed the more I did this, the less would be thrown at me. Actually at first I think more and more thoughts would come, but the more I bound them and cast them out the better it got.

After I learned how to take my thoughts captive, I found out it doesn't stop there. I guess I thought, "There, I did my part now I won't have any more trouble." I continued to meet with my pastor for about 6 months. He was teaching me how to overcome the enemy and live the crucified life, line upon line, precept upon precept. It was when I got a hold of S-R-D, that really began to make the difference. Submitting myself to God, Resisting the devil and he will flee and Drawing near to God.

There have been so many times over the years that I thought of myself more highly than I ought to and find myself in fixes that have not been fun, but it is because I am trying to be in charge of my life. I have only felt victorious when I live my life following the principles of S-R-D and living the crucified life. It doesn't matter what I am experiencing, no matter how difficult or sad or heart breaking, if I am submitted to the Lord, I have the confidence to know He will carry me through.

There was a time of real heartache in my life. I really thought I was going to die of a broken heart. My husband and I were married for a few years, and we found out we would not be able to have children. I thought my world had come to an end. All I thought about every day was that everyone else was normal and could have children except for me and my husband. I had completely lost all hope. I began to submit this area of my life to God, even though I was not sure if I could trust Him with it.

God began to drop seeds of faith and hope into my heart. This was a long process. I think if I had completely surrendered this in the beginning maybe it wouldn't have had to be so long and hard. I often use to say to God, "Why me? You know I have never asked for much, except for this one thing and yet you are withholding it from me. WHY?"

And one day it was like a light went off, and I heard in my heart, "Why not me? Look what God can do in the midst of this." So I let it go. I probably never let go completely, as I always had such a desire for children. But I did it the best way I could.

Every time I would feel sad, I would stop the thought, resist the feelings the enemy was trying to get me to embrace and surrender them to God. I would say, Oh Lord you know my desires, but I ask you to take my desires and give me yours. I would tell Him, "Kill me so I can live." I can remember pastor Bruce telling me, try laying down what you want and letting the

Lord consume it with his holy fire, and the Lord will give you beauty for ashes.

God took what little, little faith I had and He gave me not one, but two of the most beautiful little girls. I can remember thinking, who do you think you are Lori, you don't make babies, God does that. And He chooses our parents, not us. When I got a hold of that and quit listening to the lies of the enemy, what a difference. We adopted Whitney Marie from birth and five years later we got her sister Shaniya Jewell from birth. What a miracle.

Life has still not been easy at times, especially when I am trying to control it. But when I follow S-R-D, God comes through and makes all things beautiful in His time.

I will be forever grateful to my pastor for having taught me these principles. What a difference they have made in my life. I feel that without them I would be crippled.
Lori Gail

*   *   *   *   *   *   *

About 1997, not realizing my husband was in the beginning or maybe even middle stages of Alzheimer's, we were uprooted again for the fifth time in ten years. Not able to afford a home in Prescott, we bought a place in Chino Valley, Arizona. Miraculously, we found a church right there in Chino Valley – Chino Valley Word of Life. And that was exactly what it was to me. Pastor and his wife were very grounded, as were the other leaders in the church but had real personalities. I had a ball while attending there but also learned some valuable things about being a Christian.

I learned something there, that Pastor Montroy was almost emphatic about and that was the term S-R-D, which was used often in his sermons. Submit, oh how we fail to do that in our busy and practical lives. Resist, the ever busy lion, who is always roaring about and needs to be informed every day that we are able to resist him. Draw near, what a precious and tender thought. Drawing near to Jesus.

I have had to move three times since then and even had to put my husband in a nursing home in 2003, but have never been without that command, S R D.

I have been able to share that with many people but the most important aspect of those three initials has comforted and helped me go on many times since first becoming aware of how important those initials and that phrase have become in my life.

Patty Freeman

* * * * * * *

Fear has its roots in pride. I feared getting in a rut working to pay my mortgage and not producing creative work. When the fear turned to resentment and then an ungodly countenance, I had to repent. I had to submit the sinful details to God. I was not performing to the best of my ability in a part time job. That meant serving with the attitude and submission God commands in Ephesians 6:6 &7:

> *Don't work only while being watched, in order to please men, but as slaves of Christ, do God's will from your heart. Render service with a good attitude, to the Lord and not men, knowing that whatever good each one does, slave or free, he will receive this back from the Lord.*

I began to leave the house without watering "one more plant," answering one last e-mail, etc. And getting to work earlier and earlier. God had me praying not just for the cheerful and light hearted at work, but for those who have less enjoyable personality traits. I began to seek God's healing and good in the lives of others; listening more to those who were hurting, giving in time, attention and prayer.

I had to stand boldly against the enemy's attacks (resisting) when I did this. I put on God's full Holy armor every day, standing on the promise of protection in Psalm 91, for myself, neighbors, family friends and others. He brought on physical, verbal and financial attacks. Yet in pain from all three, I chose to sing praise songs, forgive myself and others and pray in belief (not double minded) that God had a purpose and a plan according to prosper and give me a vision and a hope as He said in Jeremiah 29:11-14.

On the way to work He gave me a picture of a lamb in place of the devil for my alma mater, ASU. That night I called my neighbor who took me across the highway to a family that raised Suffolk sheep. I photographed a ewe and had the maroon letters, AS, put on a cream colored T-shirt with the lamb in a dark background shaped like the letter U, to create the AS U ("EWE"

)T-Shirt. Under it is written "A Lamb on Campus." A few have sold, with the chance of more.

Most importantly, God showed me the power of His living Word. I stood on it by submitting all my detailed pride and plans, sins and fears. Then I resisted the enemy, while proclaiming God's promises out loud in praise and action (real live fruit or works). Then I joyfully drew near to God in meditative worship and acted on his promises, using his gifts with faith, and thus received His personal hug, and Holy presence.

Physical and financial healing have followed and it's an ongoing process to recall all these blessings for S-R-D to be an active formula as I walk in the spirit and truth of my Lord Jesus' example. My God submitted His own place in heaven to be a human. He resisted the devil on the mountain and drew near to His father as He died on the cross. I need to consider that often. Amen.

Laura Flood

* * * * * * *

Over the years I've talked with folks who've struggled with spouses. [Might even be that I've experienced the same.] There was a time when the end was at hand. The "d" word was spoken. It seemed impossible. Name the problem for yourself. Money woes, sexual dissatisfaction or grievances (actually it's most commonly about either money or sex... although often disguised). I've also seen physical and emotional abuse, out-of-control drug use. So difficult.

I recall one situation involving stress over both money and sex and differences of perspective on how to deal with children, where Bruce's S-R-D notion was both applicable and where it was successful. And it was so easy. Not just simple, but easy as well. At a time when either partner would very likely have sought a lawyer, one partner conversed with the Lord about the matter.

Simple? Absolutely. Ask God... with commitment to Submit to Him. That commitment is an awesome thing. Advance commitment. Just the words, "I do submit to You. Your will be done." Followed by something like, "What do I do?"

Easy? Absolutely. The still small voice saying, "Resist the devil."

In a situation like this, a person is probably committed to do what he/she said, which was submit to the Lord and obey Him. So, in silent response (silence is wise where people are nearby- people were; the time was dwindling to act in submissive obedience) the words were clear: "Satan, you're behind this entire thing. Leave."

I don't actually know what the exact words were in this specific situation, but they were not likely either arrogant or unclear. Just words of conviction. Arrogance is never appropriate for a follower of Jesus. Clarity is generally a good thing... words are most often used to communicate.

At home (much later) a hurt, confused, upset spouse asked what would happen next. "I'm not doing anything," came out. (That can't sound right.). Words also spoken with conviction, but not with animosity. "I married for life and I'm not leaving." What a silly, lame sounding response. Yet it melted an icebound situation. It began a restoration. Anger, confusion, power-playing ('kill, steal, destroy') were gone.
Professor Jerry Mason

* * * * * * *

Appendix

HOW CAN I KNOW JESUS

The Bible tells us how we can enjoy a rich, fulfilling life by knowing Jesus personally as our Lord and Savior. The Awesome Creator designed us with a capacity for love and a desire to be successful. This abundant life was formulated around mankind living in close fellowship with the Lord. Listen to the words of Jesus Christ:

Here I am. I stand at the door and knock. If anyone hears My voice and opens the door, I will come in and eat with him, and he with Me. Revelation 3:20

God's design includes provisions for us even when we're physically and emotionally drained:

Come to Me, all you who are weary and burdened, and I will give you rest.
Matthew 11:28

Yes, our loving Father God has our best in mind:

>...*I have come that they may have life, and have it to the full. John 10:10b*
>*I have told you this so that My joy may be in you and that your joy may be complete.*
>*John 15:11*

Why is it that most people are not experiencing this abundance? People have stepped out of God's plan and have tried to do their own thing. The Bible calls this sin. This rebellion blocks God's blessings from us. None of us is excluded from this problem of sin:

>*For all have sinned and fall short of the glory of God. Romans 3:23*

Some people feel that sin is an old-fashioned concept, but the Bible tells us that our sin separates us from God's blessings.

>*Surely the arm of the Lord is not too short to save, nor His ear too dull to hear. But your iniquities have separated you from your God; your sins have hidden His face from you, so that He will not hear. Isaiah 59:1,2*

Our good works and noble intentions are not sufficient to reinstate us to a standing where the holy God can bless us:

All of us have become like one who is unclean, and all our righteous acts are like filthy rags; we all shrivel up like a leaf, and like the wind our sins sweep us away. Isaiah 64:6

God's plan of salvation is the provision of His love for a race of fallen, stubborn beings. Because the Almighty is holy, His standards are essential and can't be ignored. But, because "God is love," He designed a way to reinstate those individuals who, out of sincere love for Him, would obey His instructions.

GOD'S SOLUTION

God's Spirit overshadowed a virgin named Mary, and the child that was conceived was therefore both God and man. God entered our world in human form as the son of Mary and the Son of God – Jesus, the Christ (or "Anointed One").

Jesus led a sinless life by complete obedience to Father God. Then, as our substitute, He took our place and our punishment.

Whereas the punishment for sin was death, and because He was just, God couldn't ignore sin, but He revealed in the Old Testament that He would receive a substitute payment for man's sins.

Animal sacrifices pointed to the day when God, in human form, would come to earth and be our substitute sacrifice – the Lamb of God. What God's holiness demanded, God's love provided.

For God so loved the world that He gave His one and only Son, that whoever believes in Him shall not perish but have eternal life.
John 3:16

Because Jesus was a perfect man, He could pay for our sins; because He was Eternal God, His blood paid for all who would come to Him.

Jesus willingly went to the cross and died as our sin substitute. He arose from the dead to demonstrate that God's holiness was satisfied. By rising from the dead, Jesus broke sin's power over us.

...He entered the Most Holy Place once for all by His own blood, having obtained eternal redemption... How much more, then, will the

*blood of Christ, Who through the eternal
Spirit offered Himself unblemished to God,
cleanse our consciences from acts that lead to
death, so that we may serve the living God.*
Hebrews 9:12b,14

This salvation is all of God. Going to church, doing
good works, etc., will not save us. It is very hard for
independent individuals to accept that they can do
nothing to merit salvation.

*For it is by grace you have been saved,
through faith—and this is not from yourselves,
it is the gift of God – not by works, so that no
one can boast. Ephesians 2:8,9*

OUR RESPONSE

A free gift cannot be earned, but it must be
accepted. An essential aspect of God's plan of
salvation is that it separates between those who
couldn't care less about God's will and those who,
when they see the error of their ways, will repent, or
turn from doing their own thing.

...unless you repent, you too will all perish.
Luke 13:3

I have declared to both Jews and Greeks that they must turn to God in repentance and have faith in our Lord Jesus. Acts 20:21

We receive Jesus' payment for our sin by submitting to His Lordship over our life. Submission and obedience puts us back on the original path God designed for us.

That if you confess with your mouth, "Jesus is Lord," and believe in your heart God raised Him from the dead, you will be saved.
Romans 10:9

Do you want to receive God's gift of salvation right now?

Do you believe that Jesus Christ died on the cross for your sins? That He arose from the grave on the third day?

Will you turn from being the boss of your life and surrender to Jesus, and ask Him to be your Lord?

Here is a sample prayer. Ponder it, then put it in your own words and say it to God, if you truly mean it.

Dear Heavenly Father, I come to You admitting that I have sinned and have not done Your will. I believe that, out of love, you sent Jesus, Your Son, to die for my sin. I believe that He rose from the dead and has destroyed sin's power over my life. I turn from my sin and receive Jesus as my Savior and my Lord.

The exact wording is not as important as the heart response. Did you turn from being the lord of your own life and, in receiving Jesus, are you making Him your Lord?

This may seem like a simple prayer, yet it is a legal transaction, a covenant. If you were sincere, God will honor His Word and will save you and send His Holy Spirit to live inside you.

GROWING AS A CHRISTIAN

1. Read the Bible every day. Get an easy to understand translation, such as The New International Version, The New Living Bible, or The New American Standard Bible (the translation used for most of this study).

Start reading at least a chapter a day. Begin with Matthew's gospel and read through the New Testament first; then begin reading in the Old Testament.

Make notes as you read, and write down any questions you may have to ask a Bible teacher later. Begin each Bible study with prayer for God's guidance.

Look up these verses on the importance of Bible study: 1 Peter 2:2; 2 Timothy 3:16, 17; Psalm 119:11; Psalm 1:1-3. Check the index of your Bible for the location of the books of the Bible.

2. Talk to God your Father in prayer, every day. Begin your prayer time like Jesus' example, with praise (Matthew 6:9). Confess any sin. 1 John 1:9 tells us the Lord will forgive us. Look up these verses to see what

happens when we don't confess our sin: Psalm 66:18; Psalm 32:1-7.

Pray for others (Ephesians 6:18, 19; Colossians 4:2-4). Instead of worrying, pray (Philippians 4:6-7). Give thanks in your prayers (1 Thessalonians 5:16-18). Bring your requests to the Father in Jesus' name (John 16:23,24).

3. Beware of a new pull. Our enemy, Satan, wants to pull you down, discourage you and make you give up. Jesus said the first thing that would happen to us after we receive the Word would be that Satan would come to try to steal the seed ("I didn't feel anything; nothing happened"). Also, persecution, worry, cares of this world, and the love of sin will attempt to choke the word (Mark 4:3-20).

Resist the devil in the name of Jesus the very instant you recognize his temptation traps of sin and doubt: 1 Peter 5:6-9; James 4:6-8; Ephesians 6:10-18; 2 Corinthians 10:3-5.

When temptations or pressures increase, get together with another believer. The Lord wants us to strengthen each other (Galatians 6:1,2). We're to help others. Learn all you can; share all you learn.

4. Meet regularly with other Christians (Hebrews 10:24,25). Find a good church home where the Bible is taught, God is praised, Jesus is served, and the Holy Spirit is honored.

5. Look into being baptized in water (Matthew 28:19,20; Acts 10:47,48).

6. Begin seeking the baptism of the Holy Spirit. This is when Jesus pours out the power of the Holy Spirit on us. Study these verses: Luke 11:9-13; John 7:37-39; Acts 1:4-8; Acts 2:1-4; Acts 10:44-46. Spear Ministries has a pamphlet called, "Holy Spirit Power," that deals more with this subject.

7. Begin sharing the story of God's love and salvation with others. You may be the only "preacher" some people will listen to (Romans 10:9-15).

For whoever will call upon the name of the Lord will be saved. Romans 10:13

Please share your comments with me at...

Spear Ministries, Inc.
P.O. Box 161
Prescott, AZ 86302

smi@SpearMinistries.org

www.SpearMinistries.org

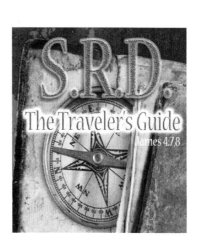

S.R.D.
The Traveler's Guide
James 4:7,8